Writing Your Story With God and *Journaling Through John* were written by Jenn Barrett.
Illustrations and cover design by Katerina Rusakova.

Copyright © 2023 by Imperfect Progress Titles
All rights reserved. No part of this publication may be reproduced in any form without permission from Imperfect Progress Titles. Requests for permission can be submitted on the form provided at ImperfectProgressTitles.com/permission.

Scripture quotations are from The ESV® Bible (The Holy Bible, English Standard Version®), copyright © 2001 by Crossway, a publishing ministry of Good News Publishers. Used by permission. All rights reserved.

ISBN 978-1-961960-00-8
First Edition, October 2023

Contents

Introduction 1
   Daily Structure 1
   Additional Tools 2
   Internal Transformation and the Life of Christ 3
   Before You Begin 3
Discussion and Review (Pre-Meeting) 7

Week 1
Day 1: Opening Image 8
Day 2: Theme Stated 12
Day 3: Setup 16
Day 4: Catalyst 20
Day 5: Debate 24
Week 1 Discussion and Review 28

Week 2
Day 6: Break into 2 29
Day 7: B Story 33
Day 8: Fun and Games--Keeping Promises 37
Day 9: Fun and Games–Momentum 41
Day 10: Fun and Games–The Bouncing Ball 45
Week 2 Discussion and Review 49

Week 3
Day 11: Fun and Games–A and B Story 50
Day 12: Fun and Games–Trajectory 53
Day 13: Fun and Games–Foreshadowing 57
Day 14: Take a Deep Breath 61
Day 15: Midpoint–Raise the Stakes 65
Week 3 Discussion and Review 69

Week 4
Day 16: Midpoint 70
Day 17: Bad Guys Close In–The "Bad Guys" 74
Day 18: Bad Guys Close In–Beginning at the End 77
Day 19: Bad Guys Close In–Bouncing A and B Story 81
Day 20: Bad Guys Close In–Tension and Momentum 85
Week 4 Discussion and Review 89

Week 5

Day 21: Bad Guys Close In–Catch Up Day 90
Day 22: All Is Lost 93
Day 23: Dark Night of the Soul 97
Day 24: Break into 3 101
Day 25: Finale–Gathering the Team 104
Week 5 Discussion and Review *108*

Week 6

Day 26: Finale–Executing the Plan 109
Day 27: Finale–The High Tower Surprise 113
Day 28: Finale–Dig Deep Down 117
Day 29: Finale–Execution of the New Plan 121
Day 30: Final Image 126
Bonus Day: Epilogue 130
Week 6 Discussion and Review *134*

Additional Resources

God's Epic Story 135
Glossary 137
Appendix 140
Dedication and Acknowledgments 141
About the Author 144
Endnotes 145
Word Count Tracker 146

Introduction

According to Joseph Epstein, 81% of Americans believe they have a book "in them." No one seems to know where Joseph got that number, but I am more curious about the second half. How is a book "in" you? And how do you get it out?

Every year nearly 500,000 people around the world take part in National Novel Writing Month (NaNoWriMo), hoping to answer that question.[1] Annually, between 10% and 20% of NaNoWriMo participants write at least 50,000 words in just 30 days![2] Yet only about 600 NaNoWriMo novels have become published books... total... since 2006![3]

So, what gives? Why this disconnect between a story burning in our hearts, getting it on paper, and publishing a book? And how do you join the group of people who successfully write their story and then share it with the world?

This guide is my attempt to help you close that gap. Through examining the plot and structure of John's Gospel, this workbook and study guide will help you pull the story "in" you onto the page. We'll also discuss topics like purpose, trust, community, and much more. The goal is to empower you to keep going through the editing, revisions, proofreading, and publication once your story is on paper.

Daily Structure

Each day we will discuss a plot point (e.g., the Catalyst) from three different perspectives. Because it most closely aligns with John's Gospel, I used the fifteen beats of the Blake Snyder Beat Sheet (BS2) to outline this study. Whenever appropriate, I included terms from other story structures.

Perspective 1: Writing Your Story

In this section, we will break down one of the fifteen beats and discuss how it could work in your story. This guide focuses on the basics; it is not a comprehensive study of plot structure.[a] It is also important to remember **there is no one right way to structure your story**. Story structures exist to provide guidelines that help you tell a more interesting story.

Books rarely follow any of these structures exactly, and yours probably won't either. Story structure provides guardrails; you must decide when your story needs to leave the highway. Use the questions in this section to explore your story as a starting place. Then let your characters, world-building, and the needs of your unique story dictate where to go from there.

As humans, we like to label things, especially each other. Two labels you will hear often in writing circles are Pantsers, people who sit down and write whatever comes to them (flying by the seat of their pants), and Plotters, who plot out every detail of their story before writing the first word. However, few people write entirely in either of these two extremes.

The impetus for this guide grew out of my failure. I "won" my first NaNoWriMo, blowing past 50k words to write more than 140k... but the manuscript lacked structure and became an unwieldy mess that I have yet to untangle into a cohesive story. This failure sent me on a journey to understand plot structure and eventually led to the creation of this guide.

Because of its origin, this guide began as a tool to help Pantsers complete the NaNoWriMo challenge with a more cohesive narrative. Thus, there are comments in many lessons about what we are "writing today." But completing each lesson before sitting down to write isn't the only, or even the best, way to use this guide. Depending on your personality and writing

---

[a] The Appendix compares four of the most popular plot structures and recommends resources for further in-depth study.

style, you may find more value by using this study to plan and outline your story, instead of while writing it. This is especially true if you connect more with the Plotter process.[a]

Perspective 2: John's Story

This section is both a case study and a Bible study. Focusing on the same story beat as before, we will examine how John used story structure in his Gospel. Before the plot analysis, there is space to record what stands out most to you in the scripture reading. This is because the lens of plot structure does not leave space to explore everything in this amazing Gospel. Don't rush through this. Give the Holy Spirit space to speak uniquely to you.

If you complete all the reading in this study, you will read the entire Gospel of John! Whether you have never studied an entire book of the Bible, or this is your 10th time through John, I hope that this study draws you closer to God, gives you new insights into the character of Jesus, and helps you experience more closely the Spirit working in your life.

Perspective 3: God's Story in Your Life

Anyone still breathing still has a purpose. If you aren't dead, God isn't done with you. It doesn't matter what you've done. It doesn't matter what's happened to you. It doesn't matter how educated you are, how articulate you are, how much money you have, or where you live. If you are still breathing, you still have a purpose. I am passionate about helping people uncover the unique purpose God has for their life.

Our third perspective on plot structure each day will examine the story God is writing with your life. You are God's "Story Worthy Hero" sent on a quest to change the world! These reflection questions provide space for you to discover your purpose and cooperate with God in living it out.

My life purpose is to *encourage, empower, and equip the sleepwalking children of God to break free of strongholds and pursue their dreams*. This study is part of that bigger purpose. Maybe your purpose is to write a book, but, like me, that could also be only a small part of the bigger picture God is painting with your life. Scripture says you are His masterpiece! Don't settle for being a bargain bin story of someone who lived and died doing nothing that matters.

Additional Tools

My hope is that you grow personally and spiritually while working through this guide. Part of that is engaging more closely with your unique personality. Some of these tools will help you and others may not connect with the way God wired you. Please don't be like me, feeling the need to fill in every blank and use every page. Use what benefits you and ignore the rest.

Daily Tracking Sheets

After each lesson, you will find a page that provides space for you to keep track of your daily goals and reflect on how each day has gone. In it, I include some of the most common daily goals, as well as space to write three more each day.

If you are working toward a specific word count goal, there is a graphic in the back of the book for you to add to each day. Before you begin, fill out your goals and rewards so you are ready to go on Day 1.

---

[a] This is also a good approach if you want to outline your story before working with a ghostwriter.

Introduction | 3

Discussion and Review

After every fifth day, I have provided questions to facilitate conversation with friends, a small group, or as a self-check along your journey. I staggered these check-ins based on a six-week study, with five lessons per week. Thus, if you are using this book for a 30-day sprint through writing a book, these will not line up with a weekly cadence.

Glossary & Appendix

I've compiled definitions for the terms in this guide into a glossary for easy reference. Throughout the study, words found in the glossary are underlined with a dashed line.

All plot structures have significant similarities because story principles are universal. The appendix has a table that compares four popular plot structures side by side to show their similarities and differences. Remember, all plot structures are simply guidelines; there is no "right" way to structure your story.

Optional Companion Journal

Throughout this guide, there are questions to help you brainstorm your story beats, dig into the Gospel of John, and explore the story God is telling in your life. Beneath each question, I provided space for you to answer. For those who want more space, I created *Journaling Through John* as a companion to this guide.

In it, you will find each day's scriptures, allowing you to highlight, mark, and scribble on them. There are also journaling pages, with lines made of the words in John's Gospel, to give you more space for your thoughts. I scattered quotes and questions from this study among the journaling pages and each entry has a full-page illustration of Jesus' story. For the sake of my eBook readers, *Journaling Through John* includes the Glossary, Appendix, and Endnotes from *Writing Your Story With God*.

Internal Transformation and the Life of Christ

Every truly successful story has both internal and external transformation. In writing circles, there are a variety of terms used, but they all agree on the purpose. The plot's external events rely on the foundation laid by an internal transformation.

We will dig more into this throughout the rest of the book, but it is important to recognize that the life of Christ is different. Jesus, being God and all, doesn't go through internal transformation. He doesn't have a misguided want that ultimately reveals a deeper need. He doesn't have a shard of glass to remove or a life lesson to learn. But if Jesus is the protagonist of John, and yet the transformation does not take place inside Him, where is it?

To answer that, we only need to ask, "What is John's theme?" Luckily, John isn't subtle about his theme. *Pisteuw*, the Greek word we translate "to believe," is in John over 100 times, half of the total uses of that Greek word in the entire New Testament![4]

Throughout John, we will see transformation take place in the people around Jesus, as they choose to believe (or reject) Him. Thus, our discussion of topics like theme, need, and B Story will focus on the transformational power of belief (or lack of belief) in the people around Jesus.

Before You Begin

Let's take a bit of time to prepare for the story you are about to write. This may appear like a daunting amount of information. Don't worry; do the best you can to fill out as much as you can, but don't get frustrated with anything you can't answer. Flag these pages for reference later. Be sure to use a pencil and be prepared to make changes!

4 | Introduction

Craft a Transformational Protagonist

We will go more into depth on these terms soon, but here is a high-level overview:
- **Theme**: the author's message to his or her audience. This usually aligns with the life lesson the protagonist must learn.
- **Problem**: what the protagonist sees as an issue in their life.
- **Want**: what they think (usually incorrectly) will solve their problem.
- **Need**: the life lesson or internal transformation that will truly solve their problem.

What is your Theme? Why are you writing this story? What is your message to the readers?

What is your protagonist's Problem?

What does your protagonist Want?

What does your protagonist Need?

If you have time, grab a journal or notebook and ask those same three questions about your key supporting characters. This guide will focus on your protagonist because their character arc carries the story's theme. But every character in your story should have their own problem, want, and need.

Identify Your Genre

You are about to write a novel! But what kind of novel will it be? Blake Snyder famously boiled down every story type to a list of ten genres. Other genre lists range from five to more than a hundred! I do my best to keep these lessons generic enough to apply to any story from any genre. Because of this, your specific genre will have variances I won't cover. Depending on your genre, readers in your target audience may also expect certain tropes. This is an area I encourage you to study further if it applies to your story.

What genre(s) best describes the story you are telling?

Are there key tropes associated with your genre(s)?

How do those tropes fit into your story?

Map Your Plotline

Explanation and discussion of each plot point makes up the bulk of this guide. For now, use this table to create a bird's-eye view of your story. Fill in what you can now. Then flag this page for reference so you can return here for a story overview as you work through the study.

Act 1	Opening Image		
	Theme Stated		
	Setup		
	Catalyst		
	Debate		
Act 2	Break Into 2		
	B Story		
	Fun and Games		
	Midpoint		
	Bad Guys Close In		
	All is Lost Moment		
	Dark Night of the Soul		
Act 3	Break into 3		
	Five Point Finale	Gathering the Team	
		Executing the Plan	
		The High Tower Surprise	
		Dig Deep Down	
		The Execution of the New Plan	
	Final Image		

Nonfiction Story Structure

I hear you now, insisting you don't need a plot because you have the cold hard facts. Your story isn't fiction; you are writing a memoir or maybe an autobiography. You don't need plot structure because you are going to share what happened when to whom and people will read it because it's true.

Unfortunately, few people will care about your story, even if it is true, unless it's engagingly written. Think about the book of John, which we are about to walk through. John had all the facts of Jesus' life. He could have written them out in a list and been done. But he doesn't do that, does he? No. He writes a story. He uses plot and structure, an Opening Image, Midpoint, Climax, Resolution, and even an Epilogue.

John isn't trying to tell us what Jesus did while he was on earth, like some first-century history teacher. The point of this story isn't to get the facts across. In fact, he even says at the end of chapter 20 that he left out lots of the details! He wants us to understand and believe that Jesus is the Lamb of God who came to take away our sins and restore us to a right relationship with God.

Whether you are writing about your life, someone else who lived, a battle that happened, or even the building of a wall,[a] take the time to make your story engaging. By all means, stick to the facts. But think about how to craft those facts into an engaging story with a protagonist who undergoes internal transformation.

Besides, if you are taking the time to sit down and write a book, there is probably a reason you want people to read it. Perhaps you believe people underestimate the pain of childhood abuse or need to trust less in technology. That is your theme, and the only way to get that theme across to your reader, the only way to change people with your writing, is to take them on a journey.

So, go back to the prior page and think about the major beats in your research. What would be the best image to open with? When does the story Climax? What or who are the bad guys closing in to stop the protagonist from succeeding? Do the best you can to fill out what you can.

I am on this journey with you, and we will get there together.

---

[a] Don't scoff. Nehemiah crafts a rather thrilling tale about this exact thing.

Discussion and Review (Pre-Meeting)

And let us consider how to stir up one another to love and good works, not neglecting to meet together, as is the habit of some, but encouraging one another, and all the more as you see the Day drawing near.
Hebrews 10:24-25

Introductions

Take some time to get to know each other.

Clarify the structure and cadence of this group going forward.

Story Check-In

Talk a bit about each of your stories, why you want to tell that story (your <u>theme</u>), and where you are in the plotting/outlining process.

Bible Study Check-In

Share a bit of your background with God (your testimony) and what you hope to gain from this study of the book of John.

God's Story in Your Life

How confident are you that God has a purpose for your life? What do you think it is?

What is holding you back from acting on what you feel called to do?

Pray and Close

Ask God to use this study to help you write your stories, grow closer to God, and better understand the purpose God has for each of you.

My notes and doodles:

Day 1: Opening Image

In the beginning was the Word, and the Word was with God, and the Word was God. John 1:1

Writing Your Story

You've sharpened your pencils, charged the laptop, and finished the outline (as finished as it will be). Today is the day we sit down and embark on this crazy journey. Over the next thirty days, you are going to write a novel! Whether your goal is 25k words, 50k words, 250k words, or just to get your story written, it all begins here.

But where is "here?" What is the first sentence? The first paragraph? How does the story start? Staring at that blank page with a blinking cursor can be daunting. You have one scene to introduce the protagonist and their problem while also setting the style, tone, and mood of the book. That's a lot of pressure to put on one scene! That pressure can sometimes make this the hardest scene to write.

A book's opening lines are critical, as they can determine whether readers will purchase and read your story. I'm guilty of spending hours, or even days, trying to settle on the perfect opening sentence to grab the prospective reader. Take a deep breath and let it out slowly. You don't need to get this perfect on the first draft. The most important part of writing your Opening Image is **writing it**. Let's talk about how.

Open your story with an Image.

The Opening Image is a single scene that draws the reader into the story by painting a picture of your protagonist in their status quo world. Save the exposition for later. How can you help your reader see, hear, smell, feel, and taste this moment? Not every sense will make it into the final narrative, but going through that mental checklist can infuse the scene with more color and vibrancy.

What sensory experiences (sight, sound, smell, taste, feel) belong in your Opening Image?

Introduce your protagonist and show us their problems.

The prep pages of this guide encouraged you to identify your protagonist's problems, wants, and needs. Don't try to set up all three in your Opening Image. Focus on introducing the reader to their problems.

Their **external problem** refers to what they believe is wrong in their life or the world. Is she lonely? Does he need a job? Has she failed out of seven colleges?

While this is before your big story-sparking-event (Catalyst, Day 4), your protagonist should still have a problem. The Midianites were oppressing Israel before the Angel appeared to Gideon. Ruth was wrestling with the loss of her husband before Naomi announced her plan to return home. And Harry Potter was suffering with the Dursleys before the letter arrived, inviting him to Hogwarts.

Their **internal problem**, or fatal flaw, references the shard of glass that they will need to remove to succeed. Does he have a temper? Is she unable to keep a secret? Does he let everyone walk all over him? While your protagonist's external problem gives you somewhere to take the story, their internal problem gives the reader something to relate to and learn from along the way.[a]

---

[a] See the Glossary for a breakdown of all these terms. I'm including as many as I can, but every plot structure uses the terms differently.

What problems (internal and external) plague your protagonist at the start of the story?

Introduce the style, tone, and mood of your book.

What is the **style** of this book? Will it be in 1st, 2nd, or 3rd person? Omniscient or limited? Reliable or unreliable narrator?[a] Contemporary language or Old English? Your Opening Image should match the style of what is coming, giving the reader an idea of what to expect as they read the rest of your story.

Tone is the attitude conveyed through sentence structure, word choice, and punctuation. Do you want the book to feel academic? Write with comprehensive vocabulary words while using precise diction and punctuation. Should this feel like reading a diary? Use less elevated language and a more casual approach to punctuation.[b]

Mood is more about the overall feel of your story. If this is a romance, the Opening Image probably shouldn't be a car chase. Use this first scene to set the overall feel of the story you want to tell.

How can you use your Opening Image to set up the style, tone, and mood of your book?

Style:

Tone:

Mood:

That is all it takes to craft an Opening Image. Create an image. Introduce your protagonist and their problems. Set the style, tone, and mood for your story. Now just put those three pieces together and you have an Opening Image. Don't worry about getting it perfect; that will come during revision! Remember, *the most important part of writing an Opening Image is **writing** the Opening Image.*

John's Story  Read John 1:1-18

What stands out most to you from John 1:1-18?

How does John make this a sensory experience?

John starts his story with Jesus (the Word) in Heaven. Jesus is with God and Jesus is God. Right away, John is laying down the foundation of his story. He is writing about the God of the universe taking on human skin to come and live among us.

But if Jesus is God, and Jesus is in Heaven with God, what is His problem?

---

[a] These terms are in the Glossary: 1st Person, 2nd Person, 3rd Person Limited, 3rd Person Omniscient, and Unreliable Narrator.
[b] Since this is more micro, you can adjust it in your second and following drafts so don't get too caught up here.

There are many "right" answers, but what stood out to me was verse 18, where John says, "No one has ever seen God." His problem relates to the separation between God and man. Jesus came to address the gap between God and His creation. He left perfection in Heaven because He is the light our world needed.

No story follows every "rule" of structure, and the Gospel of John is no different. John does not align the style, tone, and mood of his Opening Image with the rest of the Gospel. He uses this shift to contrast Jesus in Heaven and Jesus on earth. John is also making it clear from the beginning that this isn't like the other three Gospels. The Gospels of Matthew, Mark, and Luke, collectively known as the Synoptic Gospels, were all written and distributed before John. John's Gospel is distinct from the Synoptic Gospels in both structure and tone. John immediately emphasized this contrast in his Opening Image.

God's Story in Your Life

My primary goal in writing this study is to awaken you to the truth that **God has a purpose for your life, and He wants you to pursue it**! Sometimes, it's hard to see that purpose. Seasons of pain make it difficult to look past the current moment, while times of peace can lull us to sleep. We may feel too insignificant to make a difference or believe the lie that we lack the resources and connections we need to move forward. Wherever you are right now, this is just the beginning of something amazing that God wants to do!

Where does this story start? What is your "before" image?

Before we can tackle resources, connections, or even a plan, we need to find that purpose. Let's not over-spiritualize this question. We find our purpose at the intersection of our abilities, experiences, and passion. What abilities has God given you as natural talents or learned skills? What experiences have shaped your worldview and given you empathy toward people in need? What needs in the world spark your passion and light a fire in your heart? The intersection of these three questions will point a giant spotlight on your purpose.

What Purpose do you see at the intersection of your abilities, experiences, and passion?

Abilities:

Experiences:

Passion:

Purpose:

Just as books vary by style, tone, and mood, our lives each have a unique flavor created by our personalities. Are you most at home in a crowd, or do you prefer solitude and silence? Do you get caught up in the details, or do you focus on the big picture? Do people naturally follow your lead, or are you someone others feel safe confiding in? **Your personality is not a detriment to the calling God has placed on your life.** You are exactly who you need to be to do what He created you to do. God did not make any mistakes when He made you.

How does your unique personality give flavor to the purpose God has for your life?

Daily Tracking Sheet   __ / __ / __

Today's writing goal is _____, which I will celebrate by _____.

I will connect with _____, by _____.

I will move my body by _____.

Today's Personal Goals:

1:

2:

3:

Reflection Questions

Today's Biggest Victory:

Today's Biggest Challenge and How I Overcame:

I am grateful for:
1:
2:
3:

Day 2: Theme Stated

"Behold, the Lamb of God, who takes away the sin of the world!" John 1:29b

Writing Your Story

Welcome to Day 2! You made it through the hardest part: getting started. How did yesterday go? Maybe you shot out of the gate and blew past your goal. Perhaps you crawled across the finish line. Or possibly you fell short. Take a moment to really feel that elation, frustration, or failure.

Feel it? Great. Now let it go! Today is a new day. It's a new chance to make progress. Don't let yesterday's success or failure derail you.

Today we will look at the Theme Stated. Remember, the story's **theme** is what you want to tell the reader about life or the world. Typically, we communicate our theme through the **need** (life lesson) we assign to our protagonist. This need addresses the internal flaw they will overcome (or fail to overcome) in the story.

What does your protagonist need to learn?

One way we lay out breadcrumbs for readers is to have a character say this lesson early in the story (state the theme). In Gideon, the Angel of the Lord greets him by calling him a mighty man of valor.[a] Over the course of the story, Gideon will learn to trust God and, in doing so, become the person this angel describes in this declaration. In *The Help*, Constantine tells Skeeter to decide each day if she will believe what others say about her. By the end of the story, Skeeter will learn to trust herself and her own judgment instead of living the life others tell her to live.

Now is not the time to slow down the music and focus the reader's attention. The Theme Stated is a blink-and-you'll-miss-it, off-handed comment. Both the reader and the protagonist skim right by without noticing. It won't be until the end of the story, as all the threads come together, that your reader realizes you told them the theme right out of the gate.

Sometimes the theme isn't said to the protagonist directly. The theme could show up in less traditional ways as well. For example, it could be on a billboard, in a newspaper headline, on the radio, or come up in a conversation between other characters.

Who could identify this but would have their opinion ignored?

How can they tell them in a way the protagonist would believably ignore?

If the idea of already knowing your book's theme is frightening, remember it all goes back to your protagonist's internal flaw. If they have nothing to learn, the story has nowhere to go. So, have someone tell them what they need to learn. Don't let yourself get caught up trying to think of the perfect way to drop your theme into the story. This is your rough draft; let it be rough!

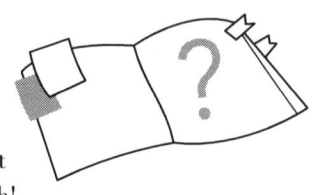

---

[a] Judges 6:12

Theme Stated | 13

John's Story
Read John 1:19-34

What stands out most to you from John 1:19-34?

Where does John state his theme?

John the Baptist is openly explaining that he is not the Messiah; he is here to point toward the coming Messiah. The next day, John sees Jesus, points Him out, and announces the theme (v29b): "Behold, the Lamb of God who takes away the Sin of the World!"

John, the disciple, is writing to prove that Jesus is the Messiah who makes a way for us to be reconciled to God. He is here to prove Jesus is God, Jesus is from God, and Jesus is the only way to restore our relationship with God. He tucks all three truths into this powerful sentence, which most of the crowd ignores!

What part of John's three points is the hardest for you to believe?

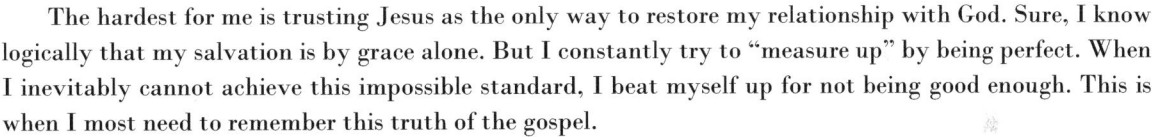

Why?

The hardest for me is trusting Jesus as the only way to restore my relationship with God. Sure, I know logically that my salvation is by grace alone. But I constantly try to "measure up" by being perfect. When I inevitably cannot achieve this impossible standard, I beat myself up for not being good enough. This is when I most need to remember this truth of the gospel.

How does knowing Jesus is God, from God, and our bridge to God affect your life?

God's Story in Your Life

Yesterday, I asked you to consider what purpose God may have for your life and how He is preparing you to change the world. Today, let's take a step back and consider what internal flaw may hold you back from that purpose.

What life lesson do you need to learn?

You may think this is easy to identify because you already feel the need to change. And your instincts may be right. But your answer may only be a symptom of the real need God wants to address in your life. Thankfully, God did not create us to live life alone. Consider who in your life may have insight into your strengths and weaknesses.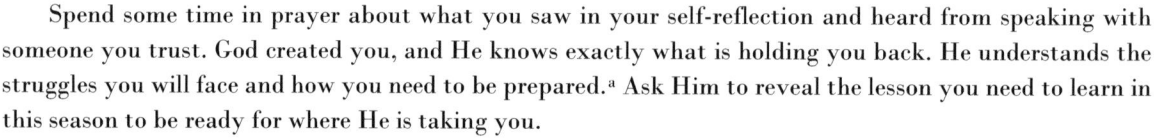

Before asking someone, consider:
- Do they know the "real" you, beyond the face you present to the world?
- Does this person want what's best for you? Are their interests in conflict with your success?
- Would this person tell you hard truths that could hurt your feelings?
- Could you receive negative feedback from this person without becoming defensive or taking offence?

Who could give insight into the life lesson you need to learn?

Spend some time in prayer about what you saw in your self-reflection and heard from speaking with someone you trust. God created you, and He knows exactly what is holding you back. He understands the struggles you will face and how you need to be prepared.[a] Ask Him to reveal the lesson you need to learn in this season to be ready for where He is taking you.

Use this space to journal your prayer.

---

[a] Read Psalm 139. God crafted every single part of you, from toenail to split end. It is in the comfort of that assurance David prays for God to search his heart.

Daily Tracking Sheet ___ / ___ / ___

Today's writing goal is _____, which I will celebrate by _____.

I will connect with _____, by _____.

I will move my body by _____.

Today's Personal Goals:

1:

2:

3:

Reflection Questions

Today's Biggest Victory:

Today's Biggest Challenge and How I Overcame:

I am grateful for:
1:
2:
3:

Day 3: Setup

"Everyone serves the good wine first, and when people have drunk freely, then the poor wine. But you have kept the good wine until now." John 2:10b

Writing Your Story

The Setup contains multiple scenes, usually covering the first ten percent of a novel. It includes both the Opening Image and Theme Stated. Tomorrow, we will leave the Setup behind as we look at the Catalyst, which will kick off your story and set your protagonist on their journey.

But why does the Setup get ten percent of a novel? That is 5,000 words in a 50k word manuscript! The Setup is where we establish why the protagonist needs to leave their status quo world to embark on whatever journey (literal or figurative) this story is about. Thus, in addition to the Opening Image and Theme Stated, there are four elements to include in your Setup.

Set up your protagonist's status quo life and show who they are as a person.

Part of introducing your main character is helping your reader see and understand who they are. Show them in various settings like school, work, home, with their boyfriend, on the playground, in the carpool line, and so on. These scenes clue your reader into your character's personality, quirks, and dreams.

Are they a realist or an optimist? Do they have 100 friends who barely know them or one friend who sees their deepest soul? Are they someone who uses humor to hide their pain or are they always the first to cry? Do they perpetually show up 20 minutes late, or are they always early?

What three places could you show your protagonist?

1:

2:

3:

How could their personality show in each?

Set up your protagonist's wants.

In our Opening Image, we hinted at your protagonist's <u>problems</u> (internal and external). In the Theme Stated, someone told them exactly what they <u>need</u> (their <u>life lesson</u>). But the Setup should also include plenty of showing us what they <u>want</u> (their <u>goal</u>). What do they **think** will make their life better?

Remember, your protagonist's wants can be (and probably are) superficial in the beginning. Perhaps they believe making more money will solve all their <u>problems</u>, ignoring their out-of-control spending. Or they think they just need to find the right boyfriend, but their crippling insecurity is attracting the wrong guys. Revisit the three scenes you listed above. In each, we should see the cracks in their status quo world and indications of their desire for change.

What does your protagonist want? What do they think will fix their problem?

How can you show their problem and goal in each of the scenes you listed above?

Set up your A Story characters.

The Setup is also where you introduce other characters who will be with your protagonist on their adventure. While some of your characters may not appear until after the Catalyst, usually there is at least one A Story (or main story) character you can introduce in the Setup. Ruth is already with Naomi before they leave for Bethlehem.[a] In *The Lord of the Rings*, Sam, Merry, and Pippen are already friends with Frodo in the Shire before the inciting incident sends them on an adventure.

What is your hero's relationship with these other characters? Are they best friends or do they barely know each other? Or maybe your story forces two rivals to work together as they face off against a shared enemy. Use the Setup to introduce other characters who will be important down the road and show their relationship with your protagonist.

Who are the important characters?

What relationship does each have with the protagonist at the start of the story?

Save the Cat!

In his first *Save the Cat!* book,[5] screenwriter Blake Snyder explained the importance of getting the audience on the protagonist's side. If your protagonist's flaws make them hard for your reader to root for them,[b] have them do something relatable or endearing to win over the audience. Blake called this the "Save the Cat" moment because the stereotype is saving a cat from a tree.

Does your character need a Save The Cat moment? What could it be?

---

[a] Ruth 1:1-5
[b] This is most often the case when your protagonist is not a traditional hero, such as a story about an antihero or a villain origin story.

John's Story

Read John 1:35-2:12

What stands out most to you from John 1:35-2:12?

What are some places John shows Jesus? How is John hinting at a need for change?

Who does John introduce? What are their relationships with Jesus?

In his Setup, John introduced us to Jesus in Heaven and then showed Him being baptized at the Jordan, gathering disciples, and attending a wedding. People are starting to "flock" around Jesus, but so far, they are the outcasts and misfits of their world. We have met some disciples, John the Baptist, and Jesus' mother. John even includes a "Save the Cat" moment by telling us about Jesus turning water into wine!

How does this miracle make you feel about Jesus?

God's Story in Your Life

God is setting you up for a great purpose! There should be indicators in your life of the purpose He uniquely created for you. Maybe you are here on Day 3, totally clear about God's purpose for your life. That's great! Perhaps you're feeling lost and don't see the connections. Don't lose heart! Continue seeking the Lord and trust that He will clarify His plan for your life.

What are some places you frequent? What do you wish would change about each?

What "side characters" has God put into your life? How might they fit into your purpose?

Your story does not have an audience to win over. No matter how broken you feel, God already loves you and is excited to work in and through you. You don't need a Save the Cat moment; God is already on your side!

Daily Tracking Sheet   ___ / ___ / ___

Today's writing goal is _____, which I will celebrate by _____.

I will connect with _____, by _____.

I will move my body by _____.

Today's Personal Goals:

1:

2:

3:

Reflection Questions

Today's Biggest Victory:

Today's Biggest Challenge and How I Overcame:

I am grateful for:

1:

2:

3:

Day 4: Catalyst

And making a whip of cords, he drove them all out of the temple, with the sheep and oxen. And he poured out the coins of the money-changers and overturned their tables. John 2:15

Writing Your Story

Can I be honest with you? I didn't want to write today. Is it alright to say that? Only four days in, and I just didn't feel like doing it. All day, I found things I would rather do… and then I did them. If you are holding this book, it means I finished writing, edited, and published! Hopefully, that encourages you to keep going when you have days like I did today.

Why didn't I feel like writing? Probably because I was too comfortable. It's raining outside, the weather is cool, and I just want to snuggle up with my cat to take another nap. Like me, your character probably doesn't want to leave their status quo life. Sure, they have wants and needs, but a bit of discomfort is preferable to the pain involved with changing. That's why today you need the Catalyst (or inciting incident) to turn their world on its head.

Bring on the pain.

The Catalyst is a moment, and it should be dramatic. In your Setup, you explained why your protagonist needs to make a change, yet they were content. Now the meteor needs to hit, dousing him in magic radiation. It's time for her boyfriend to dump all her stuff on the lawn in an uncomfortable, public breakup. This should be intense. Don't knock over their blocks; light them on fire!

The overwhelming majority of Catalysts are negative events or bad news. Even good events usually introduce pain or discomfort to our protagonist. Why is that? According to memes, we want our characters to suffer because we hate them. But that's not it. **Pain is transformational**. We act faster to avoid pain than to achieve pleasure. How long did it take you to decide what to have for dinner last night? Compare that to how long you would think before taking your hand off a hot burner.

What kind of pain does your Catalyst introduce to your protagonist's status quo life?

Ground the pain in your protagonist's greatest fear.

We talked about our main character's problem, want, and need. Another angle to view the theme is through their greatest fear, which grows from a misbelief rooted in their backstory. Perhaps she hates confrontation (fear), believing confrontation leads to pain (misbelief), because her alcoholic father abused her (backstory). Maybe he avoids commitment (fear) because he doesn't believe anyone will love him (misbelief), especially since his mother abandoned him when he was five (backstory).

Giving your protagonist an internal fear is important, but don't pick based on dramatic effect alone. Remember that your book tells two tales: the plot happens **to** your characters, and the story takes place **inside** your characters. The fear and misbelief your character struggles with should align with their internal flaw and the lesson they need to learn. These all work together to create your theme.

A diagnosis of breast cancer and the need for a mastectomy would be extra upsetting for a supermodel who struggles with her body image. No one wants to live through a breakup, but it devastates a disabled teen convinced he is unlovable.

What is your protagonist's fear, misbelief, and backstory?

Fear:

Misbelief:

Backstory:

How does the Catalyst you brainstormed stoke or exploit your protagonist's greatest fear?

Burn the boats.

In *The Art of War*, Sun Tzu taught aspiring warlords to burn the boats and bridges after crossing a border. This makes it clear to their men, and their enemies, that the only options are victory and death. Your Catalyst should be a similar no-way-back life-changing event. Ask yourself, "is there any way for my protagonist to go back to life the way it was before this Catalyst?" If you answer yes, you may need a bigger Catalyst.

Is your Catalyst big enough to make returning to the status quo impossible?

John's Story   Read John 2:13-25

What stands out most to you from John 2:13-25?

Why does this scene work as a Catalyst?

John's Catalyst is not a pain that happens to Jesus, but his first confrontation with the Jewish leaders.[a] Up to this point, others have pushed along the story. John the Baptist pointed out Jesus as the Lamb of God. Mary asked him to do something about the lack of wine. For the first time (in John's story), Jesus is instigating a direct challenge to the status quo of those around Him. You could say Jesus is the one that is bringing the "pain" by threatening the way they make money.

How does John use emotion in this scene? What does this reveal about Jesus' character?

Instead of a place of worship, this court has become filled with animal noises and bartering. These money changers and merchants also took advantage of those looking to sacrifice to the Lord, especially

---

[a] We can debate the exact placement of the 15 plot points in any story. For example, Jesus clearing the Temple also works as His Break into 2 (day 6's lesson). But John 3 fits perfectly as the Debate (tomorrow's lesson), and is near the 10% mark, making it sensible to use this scene as the Catalyst.

foreigners and the poor.[6] Jesus is "filled with zeal" (fulfilling the Psalm 69:9 prophesy), and channels that anger into action. By cleaning out the Temple the way He does, Jesus is also publicly declaring His divine authority.[7]

Ephesians 4:26 tells us to be angry without sinning. Here, Jesus gives us an example of how to respond when we feel angry about injustice without letting it drive us to sin. When confronted with injustice, it should motivate us to take action. We should not turn to gossip, complaining, or other destructive behaviors.

What injustice makes you angry? How should you react based on Jesus' example?

God's Story in Your Life

It's one thing to have a desire to see a change in the world, and something entirely different to decide to **be** that change. In big ways or small ways, God will get your attention and push you to act on the purpose He has created you to fulfill.

Sometimes God gets our attention in small, mundane ways. For instance, Christine Caine saw a wall of missing posters in an airport and the name Sophia snagged her attention. This started her journey toward founding A21, which focuses on ending modern day slavery and sex trafficking.[8] Others experience His call in more dramatic ways. After their son, Colin, drown, Janna and Jeff started Colin's Hope to help prevent other children from drowning.[9]

Still struggling with finding your purpose? Jesus became emotional when He saw the temple being used to exploit the poor and exclude the Gentiles. What injustice or need makes you emotional? Ask God to show you how to make a difference.

What has disrupted your status quo life? How might God be calling you to respond?

What is your fear, misbelief,[a] and backstory?

Fear:

Misbelief:

Backstory:

One of my greatest fears is failure because I struggle with the misbelief that what I produce or accomplish determines my value. This fear comes from a backstory of growing up with parents who made myself and my three siblings compete for attention and love. This fear of failure has often kept me from acting on the calling God has given me because I would rather not try, then try and fail.

What would it look like for you to "burn the boats?"

---

[a] You may need to "phone a friend" on this one if you don't know what misbelief you are believing. After all, it is a misbelief. But sometimes we know the lies we are believing but can't seem to overcome them, like in my example.

Daily Tracking Sheet __ / __ / __

Today's writing goal is _____, which I will celebrate by _____.

I will connect with _____, by _____.

I will move my body by _____.

Today's Personal Goals:

1:

2:

3:

Reflection Questions

Today's Biggest Victory:

Today's Biggest Challenge and How I Overcame:

I am grateful for:
1:
2:
3:

Day 5: Debate

And this is the judgment: the light has come into the world, and people loved the darkness rather than the light because their works were evil. John 3:19

Writing Your Story

Look at you; you made it to day five! Your protagonist's world has turned upside down, and now it's time to send them off on their journey. But hold on, not so fast. Your protagonist doesn't want to change; they are going to dig in their heels. The Debate is a series of scenes that give them space to process what happened in the Catalyst, decide what to do next, and prepare for the journey ahead.

Types of Debate

There are two ways to approach your Debate. The most obvious is when the protagonist debates what to do next. Your Catalyst has shaken up their status quo world, and they need time to work out how to respond. After Nehemiah learns about the problems in Jerusalem, he doesn't immediately go to the king and demand a leave of absence and supplies to build the wall. He takes time to fast, pray, and plan his next move.

In *Wheel of Time*, the three boys don't want to leave their hometown, especially since their friends and family were just attacked, and the town needs to be rebuilt. In *the Lord of The Rings*, Frodo wants Gandalf to take the ring and leave him out of it. Sometimes your protagonist doesn't have an obvious, go-or-don't-go choice. In *Divergent*, Beatrice Prior learns she is "Divergent" and can join any of the five factions, forcing her to decide which direction to take her life.

The second type of Debate is when there isn't a choice to make. Instead, the focus is on preparation and planning. There are no doubts in *Harry Potter* that Harry is going to Hogwarts. Rather than debating if he should go, Hagrid takes Harry to buy wizarding school supplies at Diagon Alley.

In the wake of your Catalyst, what major decision does your protagonist need to make?

What does your protagonist need to acquire, learn, or do to prepare for the story to come?

The Process of Debate

In the Setup, you showed your protagonist in a variety of environments, such as home, school, and work. If possible, send your protagonist back to those same places and show the impact your Catalyst made on their life. If your protagonist is instead preparing, consider thinking about the different aspects of preparation they may need. There are supplies to gather, teammates to assemble, and plans to make. This is also a great time to introduce additional A-story characters.

Remember, this is your pre-arc protagonist; they haven't overcome their fear or sorted out their misbelief. They should focus on finding a solution that lets them avoid facing their fear. Their misbelief should affect their preparation.

What are three scenes that can show your protagonist debate and/or prepare?

1:

2:

3:

How does your protagonist's fear and misbelief influence their debate or preparation?

John's Story   Read John 3

What stands out most to you from John 3?

    Multiple commentaries on John 3 say this is the most important chapter in the Gospels, or even in scripture.[a] These verses hold some of the most foundational doctrines of the Christian faith. Jesus just made a loud, emotional, and public display of claiming His divinity and authority by clearing out the Temple. Now John slows down the pace, turns down the music, and gives us space to ponder.

    John includes two scenes in his Debate. The first is with Nicodemus and Jesus, while the second is between John the Baptist and his disciples. In both cases, Jesus is the subject of debate. Through the questions of Nicodemus and John's disciples, the Apostle John asks us to ponder how we will respond to Jesus' claim of divinity and authority.

What objections do you have to Jesus' claim to divinity and authority?[b]

Nicodemus and Jesus–fear of the Light.   John 3:1-21

    In this first debate, Nicodemus comes to Jesus under the cover of darkness because he is afraid of his peers' opinions. The most famous verse in the Bible, John 3:16, is in this passage, but it's the verse that follows which was probably most transformative for Nicodemus.

    By the time Jesus is in the world, Judaism has become a religion of rules and restrictions, founded on the need to avoid God's wrath and judgment. Jesus says, "God did not send His Son into the world to condemn the world, but that the world through Him might be saved" (v17).

    This would have blown Nicodemus' mind. Jesus lays out in clear language that He has not come to point out our failings. Thank the Lord! Rather, He has come as a path to salvation. When we believe in Him, we can have eternal life.

    Jesus explains why many won't believe this good news: "People loved the darkness rather than the light because their works were evil. For everyone who does wicked things hates the light and does not come to the light, lest his works should be exposed" (v19b-20).

---

[a] "If we were asked to read to a dying man who did not know the gospel, we should probably select this chapter as the most suitable one for such an occasion; and what is good for dying men is good for us all, for that is what we are; and how soon we may be actually at the gates of death, none of us can tell." (Charles Spurgeon)

[b] Although I am a believer and have confidence in Jesus' divinity and authority, I am guilty of trying to take back that authority. Consider what obstacles hold you back from giving total control of your life and choices to God.

It is not God who condemns and pushes us into darkness. We do it to ourselves because we fear the exposing light of God's truth. This fear causes millions to reject Jesus and salvation.

What do you fear being brought into the light? How would confession bring you freedom?

John's disciples—fear of irrelevance. John 3:22-36

In the second debate, we see John the Baptist's disciples concerned about Jesus' popularity. They learn that Jesus' disciples are also baptizing, leading them to claim, "All men are coming to Him!" While this is an exaggeration, it exposes their fear of irrelevance.

John the Baptist is not concerned Jesus is drawing a bigger crowd. He knows his purpose was never to build up the name of John the Baptist, but to prepare the hearts of Israel for Jesus' coming and point to Him as the Messiah. The success of Jesus' ministry is the best possible outcome for John, who reminds his disciples that he never claimed to be the Messiah (v28).

What social pressures hold you back from submitting to Jesus' authority?

God's Story in Your Life

Maybe you feel unprepared, underqualified, or ill-equipped. Some of those objections are not obstacles; they clarify how to move forward. Marcus Aurelius said, "What stands in the way becomes the way."

What practical objections do you have to your purpose? How do these clarify your next steps?

What do you need to acquire, make, or do to prepare for the purpose God has given you?

How do fear and misbelief influence your thoughts about your purpose?

What Biblical truth contradicts your misbelief?

Daily Tracking Sheet   __ / __ / __

Today's writing goal is _____, which I will celebrate by _____.

I will connect with _____, by _____.

I will move my body by _____.

Today's Personal Goals:

1:

2:

3:

Reflection Questions

Today's Biggest Victory:

Today's Biggest Challenge and How I Overcame:

I am grateful for:

1:

2:

3:

Week 1 Discussion and Review

Let the word of Christ dwell in you richly, teaching and admonishing one another in all wisdom, singing psalms and hymns and spiritual songs, with thankfulness in your hearts to God. Colossians 3:16

Story Check-In

How is writing going?

What has gone well? What one sentence are you most proud of or want to share?

Where did you get stuck or where do you need feedback?

Bible Study Check-In

What most surprised or impacted you from this study of John 1-3?

Which "debate" from John 3 resonates most with you?

Writing Your Story with God

What purpose do you believe God has for your life?

What <u>fear</u>, <u>misbelief</u>, and <u>backstory</u> did you identify?

What is the Biblical truth that contradicts your <u>misbelief</u>?

Pray and Close

Ask God to give each of you courage to overcome your <u>fear</u>, wisdom to counter your <u>misbelief</u>, and healing to soothe the pain in your <u>backstory</u>.

My notes and doodles:

Day 6: Break into 2

The woman said to him, "I know that Messiah is coming (he who is called Christ). When he comes, he will tell us all things." Jesus said to her, "I who speak to you am he." John 4:25-26

Writing Your Story

We spent the first 20% of the novel in what's called "The Act 1 World" and now it's time to leave that world behind. The Break into 2 is a single scene that takes the story in a new direction.

Changing Worlds

Your Act 1 world and your Act 2 world need to be discernibly different. Sometimes, your protagonist will physically leave one place and go somewhere else. James and John drop their fishing nets to follow Jesus. Harry Potter boards a train and leaves the muggle world for Hogwarts. Other times, the new world is more metaphorical. Esther commits to using her influence as queen to advocate for the Jews.

Whether or not your character physically changes locations, show the reader they are leaving one world for another. Don't rush past this. The Hero's Journey calls the Act 2 world the "Upside-down World" because, in this world, everything should be the opposite of the Act 1 world.

What three things change when moving from your Act 1 world to your Act 2 world?

1:

2:

3:

Protag's gotta "ag."

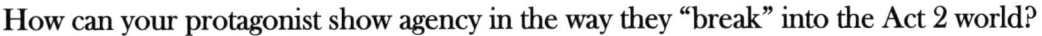

Hidden in the word "protagonist" is the Proto-Indo-European root word *ag*, which means, "to drive, draw out or forth, move."[10] The Protagonist of a story is the person who drives the story forward. This is not an event that happens to your hero; this is a deliberate move made by your protagonist.[a] In the Catalyst, you forced your hero to make a choice. They have debated, prepared, and planned. Now they are taking a decisive step.

This is the fundamental difference between the Catalyst and the Break into 2. The Catalyst happens **to** your protagonist: they are broken up with, their city is attacked by a Mongol horde, or they find out they are going to die. But the Break into 2 moment is a decisive action made **by** your protagonist.

How can your protagonist show agency in the way they "break" into the Act 2 world?

Not the right choice.

The last few days, we have discussed the importance of having a primal, deep down, soul-crushing fear keeping your protagonist from learning their life lesson. The choice they make today will **not** confront that fear. In fact, they are going to do everything they can to avoid confronting that fear and learning their lesson. Yes, they are doing something about what they want, but they are not yet reaching out for what they really need.

---

[a] This is part of what makes Twilight such a divisive story. Bella makes almost no choices; the plot happens **to** her instead of **because** of her. (The other major criticism is these books promote unhealthy relationship dynamics, but that isn't relevant to our purpose here.)

How does your protagonist's fear affect the decision they make in the Break into 2?

John's Story Read John 4:1-43

What stands out most to you from John 4:1-43?

How does Jesus break social norms in this story?

What does the woman want? What does she need? What is her fear?

Want:

Need:

Fear:

    Jesus goes through Samaria (v4) when most Jews would have gone around. He speaks to a Samaritan woman (v9). Not just any Samaritan woman; she was an outcast, unable to mingle with the other women who would go to the well in the cooler hours of the day (v6). Jesus doesn't just talk to her; he digs into the painful parts of her life that she is working to keep hidden.

    At every turn, she is changing the subject! She doesn't want to talk about her past, or the pain that has driven her to man after man. Was it infertility? Was it promiscuity? Her problem doesn't really matter; we can see her solution was to keep looking until she found the right guy. But she hasn't found the right guy; the man she is with won't even commit.

How does Jesus break into Act 2? (Hint: read verse 26.)

    This is not the first time the word "Messiah" appears in the book of John[a] but it is the first time Jesus claims this title for himself. If I was the Messiah and decided it was time to announce it publicly, I'd call up a news crew or have a meeting of the most powerful people in town. But Jesus consistently challenges our expectations. His first announcement that He is the Messiah is to a disgraced woman in a town most Jews would travel days out of the way to avoid.

Why did Jesus choose this unnamed woman[b] in Samaria to announce He is the Messiah?

---

[a] The Greek word for Messiah, Χριστός is in the Opening Image (John 1:17) and John the Baptist uses it in 1:20 (saying he is not the Messiah) and again in 3:26-30 (pointing to Jesus as the Messiah). theopedia.com/messiah-in-the-gospel-of-john

[b] Christian tradition teaches her name was Photine, she later became a missionary in Carthage, and Nero martyred her in 66AD. (orthodoxwiki.org/Photine_of_Samaria) But none of that has happened yet. Right now, she's just an outcast woman in an outcast city. Yet Jesus chooses her for His first pronouncement that He is the Messiah!

What's most baffling about this story, more even than Jesus choosing her, is what happens next. When she goes into her city, the people follow her to see who she is talking about. Her testimony (v29) is, "Come, see a man who told me everything I ever did. Could this be the Messiah?"

I'd expect a response like, "Girl, I'm no Messiah but I know all about you and what you did." But that is not their reaction. Instead, they come out to the well to see Jesus and hear what he has to say (v30). Many of them believe because of her testimony (v39). In verse 42 they say, "We no longer believe just because of what you said." This shows they initially believed based on her testimony alone!

Why do you think the people of this town listened to her? What credibility did she have?

How does their response to her story reframe your own doubts about your credibility?

When the disciples return with food, Jesus confuses them by abstaining. He claims to "have food to eat that you do not know about" and that food is "to do the will of him who sent me and to accomplish his work" (v32,34). Have you ever been so caught up in doing what you feel called to do that you forget to be hungry, thirsty, or tired? That is how Jesus feels about sharing the hope of salvation with the world. Wow, that is a powerful and encouraging picture!

God's Story in Your Life

We have talked about what may be your purpose and considered how you can plan and prepare. But today is the day. Now is the time. We all hate to do it–heck, we needed a Catalyst to force our characters into it–but at some point, we all need to take that step. Don't over-spiritualize this or think in big picture, change-the-world-someday language. Be practical and realistic about what you could do **today**.

What practical step can you take right now to live out your purpose?

How would your "Act 1 world" change into your "Act 2 world" if you took that step?

Just like our characters, we don't have the right plan the first time. But don't agonize over that right now. You cannot steer a parked car. In the same way, we need to take a step of faith, even if it's not exactly the path that will take us to the ultimate victory. Take that first step and trust God will direct you as you continue your journey.

Daily Tracking Sheet

___ / ___ / ___

Today's writing goal is _____, which I will celebrate by _____.

I will connect with _____, by _____.

I will move my body by _____.

Today's Personal Goals:

1:

2:

3:

Reflection Questions

Today's Biggest Victory:

Today's Biggest Challenge and How I Overcame:

I am grateful for:
1:
2:
3:

Day 7: B Story

When this man heard that Jesus had come from Judea to Galilee, he went to him and asked him to come down and heal his son, for he was at the point of death. John 4:47

Writing Your Story

Yesterday we broke into a new world, either physically or metaphorically. And new worlds mean new relationships, so today let's talk about the oh-so-very-important B Story and who we need to meet in this new world.[a] The most important role of the B Story character(s) is to help the hero learn their life lesson (which is the theme of your story).

Throughout the Setup, your protagonist has been in some kind of pain, but they were not willing to change. Now we meet the love interest, mentor, best friend, or rival who will do what all that pain never could: make our main character **want** to change. Not in this scene or the next, but eventually they will push your hero toward the lesson they need to learn.

What is your theme? What life lesson do you want your protagonist, and reader, to learn?

Here are three ways that a B Story character can do this. You probably won't have every type listed below, but neither are you limited to only one. Your B Story characters also don't need to be "characters." They could be animals, plants, or even an inanimate object (like the volleyball in Castaway).

The B Story character who embodies the theme.

Sometimes the B Story character teaches the theme to our protagonist because they are the literal embodiment of that theme. Despite his name in the title, V is not the protagonist in *V for Vendetta*. Eve, his pupil, is the protagonist, while V is the embodiment of the story's theme.

The B Story character who exaggerates your protagonist's flaw.

The second type of B Story character is the mirror. Do you have a bossy heroine? Enter bridezilla. Is your hero selfish? His new boss makes Scrooge look generous. Is your protagonist a coward? A member of the group is afraid of his own shadow.

The B Story character who brings out the theme in your protagonist.

Sometimes your B Story character is the force that pushes them to make a change and learn their lesson. This is where we often see romantic subplots in non-romance stories. Another common example is a mentor character, who teaches or guides them through the A Story. The mentor uses this practical role in the hero's life to challenge their worldview and help them begin the process of internal change.[b]

Who are the B-Story characters for your story?

---

[a] Before we get too far into this lesson, know that introducing your B Story characters is a part of the Fun and Games beat, which we discuss on days 8 through 14. While it is good to identify these characters now, you can introduce them anytime in the Fun and Games.
[b] Sometimes A-Story mentors fit more in the second type, exaggerating their flaw, by showing who they will become if they don't change.

John's Story

Read John 4:43-54

What stands out most to you from John 4:43-54?

John's B Story is all about the people who encounter Jesus and then choose to believe (or not to believe). While we have a few B Story characters that run throughout the book of John, he also gives us seven miracles, serving as seven case studies on belief. Back in John 2:11, we saw the disciples believe because Jesus turned water into wine. Today, we find another case study on belief, as a Roman official asks Jesus to heal his son.

John only records seven miracles in his Gospel. Seven. The Gospels include 36 miracles during Jesus' ministry. All three of the Synoptic Gospels have at least 20: Matthew–22, Mark–20, Luke–21, John–7.[11] Not only does John record significantly fewer miracles than the others, but he also records different miracles. Out of the seven miracles in John, we find only two of them in other Gospels.

Why would John choose this miracle? How does this play into his theme (belief)?

Jesus heals the son of a royal official. He's rich and probably isn't even a Jew! Here, we see belief is not only available to Jews or those who are in certain income brackets. Belief is available to all of us!

Let's look at this scene from the perspective of the man who received the miracle. He heard Jesus was in Cana, but that isn't a little jaunt into town. This man lived in Capernaum, approximately 20 miles from Cana. Depending on his mode of transportation, this is a full day, and maybe more, of traveling.

What does his willingness to travel 20 miles to find Jesus tell us about this man's desperation?

I can't prove it, but I bet this man had already tried all the healers that money could buy. His son is not just sick; he was dying. Otherwise, the man would have brought his son with him. Desperate for a miracle, this man travels all day, or possibly multiple days (especially if he had to search for Jesus). He implores Jesus to come with him to Capernaum (remember, that's 20 miles away) and heal his son.

What does this request tell us about his confidence?

How does Jesus respond? How do you think that made him feel?

Jesus rebukes the man, saying, "Unless you people see signs and wonders, you will never believe" (v48). But he doesn't argue, insisting his 20-mile trip proves he believes. Neither does he grovel or beg. He simply repeats his request that Jesus come down to Capernaum before his son dies.

Then Jesus sends him away! It feels almost dismissive. Jesus doesn't wave His hands, do an incantation, or even pray. He just tells the man to leave with an offhanded remark, "Go; your son will live."

How does this man respond to Jesus' dismissal? What can we learn from this?

The man turns to go; he knows a dismissal when he sees it. As a royal official, he's probably done his fair share of dismissing people from his presence. But he doesn't walk away downcast. Instead, John says in verse 50, "the man believed the word that Jesus spoke to him and went on his way."

Then it happens. He is still on his way home when he sees the servant coming. He probably has time to wonder if he brings good news or bad news. Does he spur his camel to find out sooner or stop and wait for the servant to reach him? We don't know. But we do know his son lives.

I am often guilty of asking for prayer and then, after God answers my prayer, never mentioning it again. This man did not do that. When he got home, he rounded up his house and told them what Jesus did. Thus, his entire household believes in Jesus.a This story challenges me to be more intentional to talk about answered prayers.

God's Story in Your Life

There are people God has put into your life specifically to walk with you along your journey to your purpose. It's probably impossible for you to sort these people into A Story (helping with your purpose) and B Story (helping you learn a life lesson). Instead, let's consider the people you already know and the people that you still need to meet.

Who is in your life right now that could help support your purpose?

How can you strengthen these relationships and invite them to join your mission?

Just like your protagonist, there are people you don't know yet who will be vital to the success of your mission. Some of these people you already know you need (a church plant needs a worship pastor) and others you may not realize you need until you meet them. Life was never meant to be lived alone.b Your purpose is too big for you to shoulder by yourself. Be intentional about seeking who God has appointed to come with you on this journey.

Who do you need God to bring to your team? (What skills, resources, or talents do you need?)

Pray for God to bring these people into your life and ask God where to look for them.

---

a The only way John would know this ending to the story is if this man, or someone in his household, became an active member of the church after Jesus' resurrection. This means they did not just believe; they lived out that faith.

b Genesis 2:18 – the first "not good" God utters about His creation is man being alone.

Daily Tracking Sheet

___ / ___ / ___

Today's writing goal is _____, which I will celebrate by _____.

I will connect with _____, by _____.

I will move my body by _____.

Today's Personal Goals:

1:

2:

3:

Reflection Questions

Today's Biggest Victory:

Today's Biggest Challenge and How I Overcame:

I am grateful for:
1:
2:
3:

Day 8: Fun and Games–Keeping Promises

"Truly, truly, I say to you, whoever hears my word and believes him who sent me has eternal life. He does not come into judgment, but has passed from death to life." John 5:24

Writing Your Story

There are only 15 beats in the BS2, and today, on day 8, we are starting the 8th. We have been sprinting through the beats! But that is because there are so many beats that hit back-to-back at the start of a story. In fact, we won't have another new beat until the Midpoint on Day 15! Don't worry if you're feeling overwhelmed or like you are falling behind.

Yesterday, we talked about the B Story, or the parallel plotline that helps your protagonist learn the theme. Today, it's time to talk about the most fun beat: the Fun and Games.

So, what kind of story are you writing? This is probably what got you excited about writing this particular story. What is that one-sentence description you fumble through when someone says, "You're a writer? What is your book about?"

- A woman travels to a world where cats are in charge and humans are their loyal servants.
- Brothers on a quest to find buried treasure.
- Childhood best friends reunite in their 80s and fall in love.

Let me tell you how you don't answer that question: with your theme. No one says, "My book is about how true love finds a way," even if that is what their 80-year-olds-in-love book is trying to say. The promise you make to readers who pick up your book and read the back is what we get to see in the Fun and Games.

Readers picked up the *Hunger Games* to read about children fighting to the death. The Fun and Games starts when Katniss comes out of that tube into the battlefield. *Harry Potter* promised a story about learning to use magic, so the Fun and Games includes classes on charms and flying on broomsticks.

What do you promise your readers with your book's premise?

The most important part of your Fun and Games beat is that it keeps this promise to your reader. Yes, you need tension, trajectory, character development, and all the rest of that (which we'll talk about in the coming days). But if you don't keep the promise you made in your premise, readers will feel misled. And readers who feel misled rarely leave raving reviews or refer your book to their friends.[a]

Thinking about your promise, what are 3-5 scenes you need to include in your Fun and Games?

1:

2:

3:

4:

5:

Often these are the scenes that made you want to write this story. Now the question becomes how you tie all these scenes together. That is what we will look at over the next several days. For now, start getting these scenes on paper!

---

a I am aware there are exceptions. Sometimes the entire book is a twist on the premise. But this should be undertaken with extreme care.

John's Story   Read John 5

What stands out most to you from John 5?

John's premise is most clearly stated in John 20:31. He wrote his Gospel to prove that Jesus is the Messiah, and that life is available to those who believe in Him. In this chapter, we see three ways Jesus claims divinity. He heals a man who couldn't be healed, He claims divine authority, and He identifies five "testimonies" about Himself.

Jesus heals the unhealable man.   John 5:1-15

Like we talked about yesterday, John only records 7 of Jesus' miracles, and each of them is unique in what they teach us about God. So far, we have seen Him turn water into wine and heal someone 20 miles away. Here we see him take on a new challenge: healing a man who may not want to be healed.

What is strange about the question Jesus asks (v 6) and the man's response (v7)?

This man has been an invalid for nearly four decades and Jesus asks him if he **wants** to get better?!? This is such a bizarre question. And the man's response is even more strange. Instead of shouting "yes" at the top of his lungs, he makes an excuse for why he hasn't gotten well yet.

In thirty-eight years of living as an invalid, the man's identity is now tied to his affliction. Jesus asks if he wants to let that identity go. "Do you really want to get well?" The man responds from his broken identity with his well-worn excuse for why he can't. "It's not my fault; I don't have help."

Jesus doesn't refute his excuse. He doesn't insist the man could have figured it out if he really wanted to. Instead, Jesus invites him to choose a new identity. Jesus commands him in verse 8 to get up and walk. The only way this man can obey Jesus is to let go of the broken identity and act in obedience.

This affects me every time I read John 5. But it was especially meaningful when I first heard Craig Groeschel explain it in a Life Church podcast. For years, I'd battled with the same sin. My failure to win that battle had become my identity. In that moment, I heard Jesus ask, "Do you **really** want to get well?"

What broken identity have you held on to? Do you really want to get well?

Jesus claims divine authority.   John 5:16-30

The Jewish leaders became enraged because he healed a man on the Sabbath, the day of rest. The Sabbath is a consistent source of tension between Jesus and the religious leaders. But this may be confusing to those of us in the western world, far from Jewish traditions. The Jews had two scriptures:

- **Written Torah**: this is the first five books of the Bible and is God's message to the Jews about how to live.
- **Oral Torah**: about fifty times as long as the Written Torah, this is the word-of-mouth tradition passed down for years on how to interpret what God said. The Rabbinic tradition teaches that the Oral Torah is more vital to righteous living than the Written Torah.[12]

In Exodus 20:8-11 we are told to keep the Sabbath as a day of rest (Written Torah). Along the way, the Oral Torah defined what it means to keep the Sabbath, and these rules grew more and more restrictive with time. It blew my mind to discover there are special elevators in Israel that "true" Jews use on the Sabbath![13]

Jesus argued with Jewish leaders about the Sabbath to expose how they valued their traditions over loving God and people.[14] Their religion had become their God.

How have your religious preferences become a barrier to loving God or loving others?

Jesus identifies five testimonies about Himself. John 5:31-47

What are the five "testimonies" Jesus claims prove His authority?

v33-35:

v36:

v37-38:

v39-40:

v45-47:

What can you learn from His rebuke in v41-47? Where is your hope set (v45)?

Jesus points to the testimony of John, His miracles, the Father, the Old Testament, and Moses. Despite all this evidence, they do not believe because they love their position, wealth, and tradition more than they love God. They criticize Jesus for not following God's commands, claiming that obeying The Law proves their love for God. But Jesus rebukes them for not loving God (v42) but the praise of man (v44). They set their hope on the Law of Moses; but Moses was writing about Jesus!

How does John keep the "promise of the premise" in today's reading?

Writing Your Story with God

When we embark on the journey living our purpose, we usually begin with a feeling of optimism and excitement. In the days to come, we will discuss how to handle challenges when they arise. For today, let's focus on what is exciting about your purpose.

What most excites you about your purpose?

Daily Tracking Sheet

___ / ___ / ___

Today's writing goal is _____, which I will celebrate by _____.

I will connect with _____, by _____.

I will move my body by _____.

Today's Personal Goals:

1:

2:

3:

Reflection Questions

Today's Biggest Victory:

Today's Biggest Challenge and How I Overcame:

I am grateful for:

1:
2:
3:

Day 9: Fun and Games—Momentum

And a large crowd was following him, because they saw the signs that he was doing on the sick. John 6:2

Writing Your Story

Welcome to the second day of working on your Fun and Games. According to Blake Snyder, the Fun and Games is about 30% of a story, or roughly 15,000 words in a 50k novel. The good news is this length allows the reader to explore your world. However, the downside can be a lack of tension and direction.

On Day 12, we will discuss trajectory, so we won't spend much time on that today. But ultimately, your story needs to have movement. This is where many of my best world-building ideas have died as unwritten stories. No matter how interesting I make the world, to keep the reader engaged and turning pages, something needs to happen.

Momentum doesn't only mean having a plot; it is about creating a feeling the plot is advancing toward a destination. Depending on the type of story you're telling, this can sometimes be straightforward. If you have a group of adventurers on a quest to collect the magic MacGuffin, momentum comes from your characters physically moving toward their goal. Books that span a school year can show progress through tests, report cards, and movement toward an event, like prom or graduation, at the end.

If you've studied plot structure before, you know the Fun and Games is driving toward the Midpoint. Although we will discuss the Midpoint on days 15 and 16, a rough idea of what it means for your story will make writing momentum in your Fun and Games significantly easier. Are you moving toward the first kiss, or is the wedding closer to your Midpoint? Will they find the MacGuffin at the Midpoint, or is that saved for closer to the Climax?

Where is your story going? What happens at the Midpoint?

Midpoints don't come out of nowhere; they need buildup. If the Midpoint is a first kiss, the Fun and Games part of your story should show the relationship growing from the meet cute in your Catalyst. Stories about completing a quest should have stops along the way to help create a feeling of progress on that quest.

What 3-5 events show progress toward your Midpoint?

1:

2:

3:

4:

5:

How do these events align with the promise-keeping scenes you brainstormed yesterday?

John's Story   Read John 6:1-21

What stood out to you most from your reading of John 6:1-21?

The two miracles in today's reading are the only miracles John records that are also found in the Synoptic Gospels. In fact, Jesus miraculously feeding 5,000 people is the only miracle recorded in all four Gospels (aside from the resurrection). There must be something important about this specific miracle!

Feeding the Five Thousand   John 6:1-15
Also, Matthew 14:13-21, Mark 6:30-44, and Luke 9:10-17

Why do you think all four Gospels record this miracle? What does it tell us about Jesus?

Read one or more of the other three. What is unique about John's version? What's similar?

All four Gospels begin this story with Jesus pulling His disciples away, but the crowd still finds them. Jesus makes space for the spiritual and physical needs of these people who are seeking him out. Interestingly, John's is the only Gospel to mention the boy, and his faith, although all four speak of five loaves and two fish. Also, John's retelling is the only one with the lens of a future perspective.[a]

Walking on water   John 6:16-21
Also Matthew 12:22-33 and Mark 6:45-52

What does this miracle tell us about Jesus?

Read the Matthew and/or Mark passage. What is unique about John's version? What's similar?

In all three Gospels, this story comes after Jesus feeds 5,000 and then sends the disciples on ahead. Also, in all three, a miracle occurs when Jesus enters the boat, although only in John is this miracle immediately arriving at their destination. Only in Matthew does Peter walk on water, and only Mark claims Jesus intended to walk by them.

How does John create a feeling of forward momentum in today's reading?

---

[a] John 6:6 – "He asked this only to test him, for he already had in mind what he was going to do." The other Gospels use a more fact-based lens (what happened) instead of this reflective lens (why it happened).

Jesus is becoming more popular, and people are following Him wherever He goes, showing progress in the A Story. This growing influence will eventually push the religious leaders to arrest and crucify Him. The B Story, people believing in Jesus, will become more prominent in the second half. But we can already see B Story progress in the boy's faith and how the disciples react to Jesus calming the sea.

God's Story in Your Life

Just like the page-turning power of momentum in stories, progress keeps us motivated to work toward our purpose. When we make progress, it's easier to stay excited and engaged.

Taking consistent action leads to small successes. These little achievements may not have a major impact, but they encourage us to continue our efforts. Because we keep doing the work, we experience bigger successes, triggering a compounding effect. This is why daily habits are so powerful! They build routines that create momentum.

The same is true for poor decisions, which compound in a negative direction. Skipping my time with God for one day doesn't seem important. But after a few days, I will start feeling further from God. As that gap grows, it becomes harder to motivate myself to spend time with God, because I don't feel His presence or hear the Holy Spirit's call.

Look back at your purpose. Yes, there are some bigger milestones along the way, but let's identify one daily habit that can help you build momentum. This habit should be something so small it is easy to do every day, even on your worst day. Maybe it's writing one sentence, opening the Bible App, or sending an encouraging text to someone on your ministry team.

Often that little step gets you started, and you are on your way. (After all, who wants to write just one sentence?) However, on hard days, you can celebrate that you kept your promise to yourself.

What simple habit can help you build momentum toward your purpose?

Great, now go do it!

Tomorrow, we will look at addressing setbacks. For now, focus on following through with the habit you identified. If you kept it simple, you can do it today! If you can't, your habit may be too difficult to commit to, which will keep you from building momentum. Consider scaling it back to something simpler you can commit to do consistently.

Please note: "Consistently" isn't necessarily synonymous with "daily." I strive to swim in the morning four to five times a week. It also isn't about beating yourself up when you fall short. Recently I was sick and didn't go at all for two weeks! The balance between committing to small goals and showing self-compassion when you miss the mark can be tricky. If this is an area of weakness for you, prayerfully read through Proverbs, which teaches a healthy balance on both sides of that line.

Daily Tracking Sheet   ___ / ___ / ___

Today's writing goal is _____, which I will celebrate by _____.

I will connect with _____, by _____.

I will move my body by _____.

Today's Personal Goals:

1:

2:

3:

Reflection Questions

Today's Biggest Victory:

Today's Biggest Challenge and How I Overcame:

I am grateful for:
1:
2:
3:

Day 10: Fun and Games—The Bouncing Ball

"From this time many of his disciples turned back and no longer followed him." John 6:66

Writing Your Story

Have you ever read a book with momentum that was still boring? Maybe you struggled through and finished it. Or perhaps it was so bad you wrote it off as a DNF (Did Not Finish). Possibly, like me, you left it in your perpetually growing "current reading" pile and started reading something else. Books are easy to put down and hard to resume reading when they lack tension.

To maintain tension, aim for a "bouncing ball" structure with events that alternate between progress and obstacles. Think about all those motivational posts you see on social media. The path from inciting incident to Midpoint shouldn't be a straight line.

For example, the protagonist has a great first date (progress). But then, he doesn't text or call for a week (obstacle). He wins her back by surprising her with 100 roses (progress). Later she catches him at a restaurant with another girl and stops answering his calls (obstacle) until he corners her to explain it was his cousin (progress). This will-they-won't-they keeps the reader hooked to find out what happens next.

A questing team deciphers the clue from the inciting incident (progress). But there is a troll guarding the bridge (obstacle). They find another way across the river (progress), but a member of the party breaks his leg (obstacle). They meet a shaman who heals the broken leg (progress) then steals their map (obstacle).

Look at what you've written so far, plus the scenes you have planned, and make a list of all the events that make up your Fun and Games. (Consider events, not scenes; a single scene may include multiple events.) Categorize your events as progress or obstacles, then consider rearranging or adding scenes to maintain a bouncing ball of tension.

Here is a table to help you map out the bounce in your Fun and Games:

Progress	Obstacle

Day 10

John's Story   Read John 6:22-71

What stands out most to you from John 6:22-71?

How does John show a "bounce" in today's text contrasted with yesterday?

Talk about a bouncing ball! Yesterday, Jesus was giving everyone food without being asked. Today, He's calling out those same people for only wanting physical food. Yesterday, He had people seeking Him out, even when He tried to pull away. Today, those same people are deserting Him because of His hard sayings.

Seeking God's hand instead of His heart.   John 6:22-34

Why does Jesus rebuke the crowd in v26-27? What's His point?

What is the crowd's response (v 30-31 and again in 34)?

Jesus rebukes the crowd for only following Him because He gave them bread and fish. He tells them they should, instead, believe in Him, as the one God sent (v29). But they respond by asking Him for more bread! The crowd is more interested in Jesus meeting their physical needs than the spiritual needs He came to satisfy. Like them, we can be guilty of seeking the "hand" of God (material provision) instead of the "heart" of God (relationship).

Consider your recent prayers. Have you prioritized God's "hand" over His "heart?"

Hard truths and difficult sayings   John 6:35-71

What are some of the hard truths Jesus shares in this passage?

What rebuttals do we see from the crowd?

Jesus claims to have come from Heaven, but many of these people know Jesus as Mary and Joseph's son. They are also disgusted by the image of eating Jesus' flesh and drinking His blood. Today we can look back and know Jesus is talking about the Lord's Supper, but we should remember that these people didn't have that context.

In v66 we read many disciples turned away. What does v44-46 tell us about this?

What hard truths have made you want to turn away from obedience to God?

After the crowd deserts, Jesus turns to the disciples and asks if they want to leave too. Then in verse 70, He mentions Judas will betray him. While there is no way to know for sure, I think it sounds like He's feeling down. For me, that's very encouraging. Even Jesus experienced disappointment!

God's Story in Your Life

The path to success is never a straight line. Life is messy and people are complicated. Sometimes we get off track and miss a day, or a week, and struggle to start again. Other times, people or systems block our progress and make it harder to move forward.

What are some obstacles to your Purpose?

How can you keep moving forward anyway?

Cindy Hawks spoke at a women's conference I attended several years ago. She talked about how, when we fail, we don't start over. Instead, we start moving in the wrong direction. This means the sooner we turn back around and start going the right way, the more progress we will make and the faster we will reach our goals. Wherever you are, whatever you did or didn't do yesterday, pick yourself up today and take at least one step forward on your purpose.

How can you "get back up" when you make a mistake or lose momentum?

What keeps you motivated?

Daily Tracking Sheet

___ / ___ / ___

Today's writing goal is _____, which I will celebrate by _____.

I will connect with _____, by _____.

I will move my body by _____.

Today's Personal Goals:

1:

2:

3:

Reflection Questions

Today's Biggest Victory:

Today's Biggest Challenge and How I Overcame:

I am grateful for:
1:
2:
3:

Week 2 Discussion and Review

"For where two or three are gathered in my name, there am I among them." Matthew 18:20

Story Check-In

How is writing going?

What has gone well? What one sentence are you most proud of or want to share?

Where did you get stuck or where do you need feedback?

Bible Study Check-In

What most surprised you from John 4-6?

How have you been guilty of seeking God's "hand" instead of His "heart?"

God's Story in Your Life

What action did you take, or habit did you start, to build momentum toward your purpose? If you didn't, when will you?

How do you keep going when you face resistance or setbacks?

Pray and Close

Ask God to help you stay committed to your daily habits.

Pray for God to bring the right people into your lives to support your individual purposes.

My notes and doodles:

Day 11: Fun and Games—A and B Story

And there was much muttering about him among the people. While some said, "He is a good man," others said, "No, he is leading the people astray." Yet for fear of the Jews no one spoke openly of him. John 7:12-13

Writing Your Story

Wow, look at everything you have done to put together an amazing A Story! You have momentum. You have tension. Everything is coming together. But don't forget, you are telling two different stories:

- **A Story**: this is the plot of your story (find the MacGuffin)
- **B Story**: this is the internal transformation of your story (learn the value of friendship)

Remember, your B Story has its own characters, or different relationships with the same characters (like we talked about on Day 7). Today, we'll focus on the influence your B Story has on your A Story in this part of your book, before they become intertwined by the Midpoint.

At the Midpoint, you will raise the stakes, usually with a False Victory or a False Defeat. Your B Story should be the reason your A Story doesn't end at the Midpoint. In the Fun and Games part of your book, the protagonist is acting to pursue what they want while avoiding the internal change they need. They are pursuing the girl without overcoming their selfishness. They are going after the MacGuffin without trusting their fellow adventurers. When you think about your story like this, integrating your A Story and B Story is much easier. Progress happens despite not learning the theme, while failures come because they haven't learned the theme.

Let's imagine a story about Travis falling in love with Sarah while battling a drug addiction. When they break up, it's because he got high after school and forgot about their plans, leaving her waiting for hours in the park for him to show up. When he wins her back with chocolates and roses the next day, he isn't addressing the real problem (his addiction), so the progress is going to be temporary.

What is your protagonist's flaw? What life lesson do they need to learn?

Think about the scenes you listed yesterday for your Fun and Games. The places where your protagonist makes progress, they should succeed despite not learning this lesson. Where they are failing, they should fail because they refuse to address this flaw.[a]

How is your protagonist's flaw shown in the way they make progress?

How can you use your protagonist's flaw to trigger or amplify obstacles?

---

[a] Note: their internal flaw may not cause every obstacle. But it should influence how they respond to those challenges.

Fun and Games | 51

John's Story
Read John 7:1-24

What stands out most to you from John 7:1-24?

How do we see A Story (path to the cross) in this passage?

How do we see B Story (people believing or rejecting Jesus) in this passage?

What does verse 13 tell us about the religious climate? How does this play into the B Story?

Jesus progresses the A Story by "ruffling feathers" and speaking openly. His growing popularity and willingness to speak against the religious system is kindling hatred and fear in the religious leaders. Eventually, they will call for His crucifixion. The B Story shows up in the whispered conversations of people throughout this passage. Despite wanting to believe, the crowds are unwilling to support Jesus because they fear the Jewish leaders.

In verse 21-24, Jesus points out the hypocrisy of their Sabbath rules. They circumcise babies on the Sabbath, to fulfill their religious rituals, but became angry when He healed someone on the Sabbath. Jesus is showing that their religion is more important to them than compassion, which God wants more than their ritualistic obedience.

What routines or rituals keep you from loving people well?

God's Story in Your Life

Take some time to look back on the life lesson you identified on Day 2. Consider how God has helped you progress in this area while working toward your purpose.

How is this life lesson intersecting with the purpose you are pursuing?

Like the stories we write, our lives have multiple parallel plotlines. This study has focused on God's bigger purpose for your life. But while you embark on your purpose, you are still a mother, father, wife, husband, son, daughter, friend, employee… the number of plotlines is endless.

God doesn't want each area of your life (work, church, school, home) to be isolated in its own space. We are not called to be Christians on Sunday and then set that plotline aside to embrace another on Monday morning. If God is working in one area of your life, it will affect all the other plotlines as well.

How may your purpose impact other areas of your life?

Daily Tracking Sheet

___ / ___ / ___

Today's writing goal is _____, which I will celebrate by _____.

I will connect with _____, by _____.

I will move my body by _____.

Today's Personal Goals:

1:

2:

3:

Reflection Questions

Today's Biggest Victory:

Today's Biggest Challenge and How I Overcame:

I am grateful for:
1:
2:
3:

Day 12: Fun and Games–Trajectory

So there was a division among the people over him. Some of them wanted to arrest him, but no one laid hands on him. John 7:43-44

Writing Your Story

Hey, look at you, halfway through your Fun and Games, and you haven't given up yet! So far, we have discussed keeping our promises, maintaining momentum, creating tension, and integrating A Story and B Story. Today, we will explore the overall direction of your Fun and Games.

There are two general approaches to trajectory in the Fun and Games: Onward and Upward or Floundering Forward. Before you can know which of these two applies to your story, you will need to think again about your Midpoint. There are two types of Midpoints:

- **False Victory**: The protagonist thinks they have achieved the goal, but they have not.
- **False Defeat**: The protagonist thinks they have failed and cannot succeed, but there is still hope.

The "false" part of each is because your Midpoint will fall only halfway through your story. We will look more at these when we reach days 15 and 16, so don't worry too much about the specifics. That said, we need to identify which direction your story is going. If you are writing a love story and the Midpoint is a first kiss (victory), you are writing with a positive trajectory. If, at the Midpoint, the female protagonist becomes engaged to the wrong guy (defeat), it's a negative trajectory.

Onward and Upward.

This type of story structure is all about stories that move on an upward path, leading toward a False Victory at the Midpoint. While you still need progress and obstacles (bouncing ball), the overall movement is in a positive direction. The couple has ups and downs, but they are growing closer together. The quest has good days and bad days, but the team is making progress toward their goal of finding the MacGuffin. Whatever the story, the protagonist experiences bigger wins and smaller losses, moving the story in an overall positive direction.

Notice I said "bigger" instead of "more." You still want to use the bouncing ball to create tension, so you will have around the same number of progress and obstacle events. Rather than having more successes than obstacles, your successes should be more significant than your obstacles. Think of this as taking two (or three) steps forward and one step back. Overall, your characters move forward.

Floundering Forward

Notice I called this "Floundering Forward," not "Falling Backward." This is because we want to maintain momentum, even when the protagonist feels like everything is going wrong. Stories in this category are moving toward a False Defeat for their Midpoint.

The couple's on-again-off-again romance seems to go all wrong and, by the Midpoint, it appears they will never make it work. For every success on their quest, the group encounters an even bigger obstacle; by the Midpoint, they are prisoners in the lair of the Dark Lord.

Like stories with positive trajectories, these should still have a mix of progress and obstacles. But in these stories, the progresses are smaller and the obstacles bigger, creating an overall negative trajectory.

What will be your Midpoint? Is this a victory or a defeat for your protagonist?

On your list from Day 10, score each from 1 to 10 based on how much they move the story.

There isn't a right or wrong way to do this. How many steps forward or backward would you consider each event? I know it's no fun, but let's do some quick math. Add up the totals for each of the two categories (obstacles and progresses). If the resulting number is too small,[a] your readers may feel like there isn't enough progress being made, causing you to lose momentum.

- **Onward and Upward**: subtract the obstacle score from the progress score. If this number is too low, increase the impact of your progresses and soften the setback of your obstacles.
- **Floundering Forward**: subtract the progress score from the obstacle score. If the number is too low, make your obstacles more destructive and your progresses less impactful.

What can you do to have more trajectory?

John's Story   Read John 7:25-52[b]

What stands out most to you from John 7:25-52?

What kind of trajectory do you see in John? Why?

This section has a considerable amount of bounce! There is the will-they-won't-they about arresting Him and questions about if the people will believe. Still, John's Gospel has an overall positive trajectory; Jesus is making steady progress both in the A Story (walking toward the cross) and in the B Story (more and more people believing in Him).

The declaration in verses 37-38 has far more significance if you take the time to understand the historical context of this passage. Jesus is speaking on the last day of the seven-day Water Liberation Ceremony, which is a part of the Feast of Tabernacles. Here is an explanation from Jewishroots.net:

> This outpouring is to take place during the days of the Messiah, the anointed one, a descendant of King David, through whom salvation will come to Israel. Based on Isaiah 12:3, the Pool of Siloam became known as the "well of salvation" and was associated with the messianic age. Thus, to the Jewish people of the Second Temple days, pouring water on the altar at the Feast of Tabernacles was symbolic of the Holy Spirit poured out during the days of the Messiah.[15]

How does this context change your understanding of John 7:37-39?

---

[a] If you get a negative score, reconsider your trajectory. Maybe your thought this was a Floundering Forward story but it's more Onward and Upward than you realized.

[b] We will not be covering John 7:53-8:11 because it is not in the original manuscripts. The earliest versions of John that includes this story are from 500 AD. There will be time during the Week 3 Discussion and Review to discuss this story and how it fits into the overall narrative of John.

Do "rivers of living water" flow from you?

What does this look like practically in your life?

God's Story in Your Life

How do you feel about the story God is writing with your life?

Is it trending up or down?

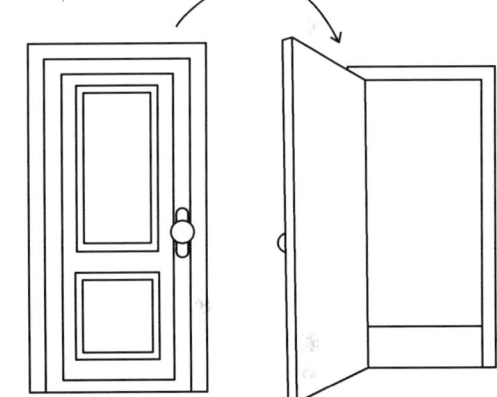

Sometimes, what feels like a setback can actually be a setup. Jesus experienced the ultimate setback when they arrested and killed Him, but it all turned out to be a setup for the resurrection. Without that setback, His mission, to provide us a way back to God, would not have been possible.

Likewise, in our lives, it can feel like we've hit obstacles that halt our progress. Don't lose heart! Over and over again, I've noticed proof that God was working in the background all along. Even though we may not understand His ways, He remains faithful.

When it feels like one door is slamming in your face, look around to see where God is opening another. Find encouragement in Romans 8:26-30. God is using the situations in your life to transform you into the image of Christ. He is not a quitter and will finish what He started.

What setback feels like it's pushing your purpose backward?

How might God turn that setback into a setup that puts your purpose back on track?

Daily Tracking Sheet

___ / ___ / ___

Today's writing goal is _____, which I will celebrate by _____.

I will connect with _____, by _____.

I will move my body by _____.

Today's Personal Goals:

1:

2:

3:

Reflection Questions

Today's Biggest Victory:

Today's Biggest Challenge and How I Overcame:

I am grateful for:
1:
2:
3:

Day 13: Fun and Games—Foreshadowing

"I told you that you would die in your sins, for unless you believe that I am he you will die in your sins."
John 8:24

Writing Your Story

Yesterday we discussed trending your Fun and Games toward a False Victory or False Defeat. Today we are going to talk about the "false" part of that victory or defeat. At the Midpoint, most stories change directions. This is the infamous "Midpoint twist."

Your lovebirds kiss for the first time... then she learns he is the son of the man who killed her father. Or maybe your midpoint is the wedding... after which he discovers he's her fifth rich husband, and the other four died shortly after the honeymoon.

Your questing team finds the magic MacGuffin... then discover it's been replaced with a fake. Or maybe they find the true MacGuffin... but it's immediately stolen by the bad guy, who joined the party disguised as a shaman, back when someone broke their leg.

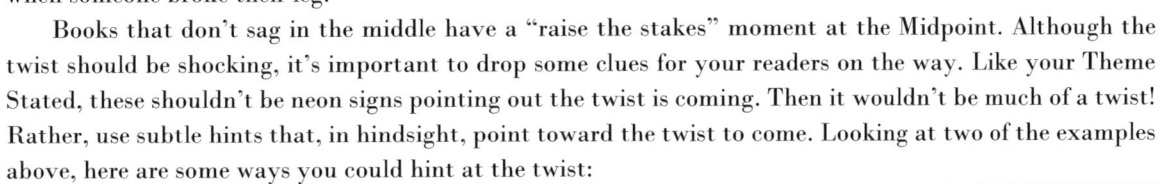

Books that don't sag in the middle have a "raise the stakes" moment at the Midpoint. Although the twist should be shocking, it's important to drop some clues for your readers on the way. Like your Theme Stated, these shouldn't be neon signs pointing out the twist is coming. Then it wouldn't be much of a twist! Rather, use subtle hints that, in hindsight, point toward the twist to come. Looking at two of the examples above, here are some ways you could hint at the twist:

Midpoint	Twist	Foreshadowing
The two get married	He's her fifth rich husband and the other four died shortly after the wedding.	• She lacks backstory or seems almost too perfect. • She has a lot of nice things but works as a barista. • He has a lot of money, and she enjoys spending it.
Find the MacGuffin.	Immediately stolen by the bad guy, who disguised himself as a shaman and joined their party to fix someone's broken leg.	• Someone mentions how lucky they were a shaman was wandering in the woods so far from any towns. • An animal companion never stops growling at him. • He never takes off his pack or wanders the camp at night.

What twist might you use to "raise the stakes" at the Midpoint?

What are some ways you can foreshadow the coming "raise the stakes" moment?[a]

---

[a] If you don't know what this "twist" will be yet, that's alright. Keep writing and you can come back and add in these details later.

Remember, these are not entirely new scenes. Instead, they are subtle anecdotes, comments, or apparent inconsistencies. Right now, they slip by, but in retrospect, or on the second read through, they will make sense to your reader. If you are struggling with ideas, look over your existing list of scenes and consider how the coming twist would affect the interaction.

Ask yourself questions like:
- What does she know the person she's pretending to be wouldn't know?
- What doesn't he know that should be obvious to his persona?
- What might this person accidentally say while drunk or in their sleep?
- How does this organization controlling things from behind the scenes impact the world-building?

One other important factor to consider is your audience. If you are writing for Middle Grade or Early Readers, you probably will need more heavy-handed foreshadowing. But if your audience is adults, then you want it to be more subtle.

John's Story   Read John 8:12-47

What stands out most to you from John 8:12-47?

How does John foreshadow the cross to come?

To me, the most obvious foreshadowing in John is the reframe, "…because His time had not yet come." They are constantly trying to stone, seize, arrest, and kill Jesus. John continually emphasizes that Jesus will suffer and die, just not yet.

A point of pride for the Jewish leaders was their pure lineage. They would trace their ancestors back to the original 12 tribes[a] and point to Abraham as their father. I want to **briefly** explain a bit of context. God called the Jews to live lives set apart as His holy people.[b] This was not to exclude the other nations, but to be a light for all nations to find God.[c] Unfortunately, the Jews believed this meant they were superior and created a very xenophobic view of the rest of the world[d] (which they called Gentiles).[16] These Jewish leaders are confident of their position with God because they are descendants of Abraham.

How does Jesus dispute their claims to be Abraham's children and God's children?

---

[a] Paul later lists in Philippians 3:4-6 the reasons he is "winning" by Jewish standards. (He then goes on in verse 7 and 8 to say that those standards are worthless.) Having Benjamin as his ancestor is part of this list.

[b] Way too many references here to list them all but here are a few: Deuteronomy 7:6-8, 26:19, and 28:9.

[c] Way too many references here to list them all but here are a few: Isaiah 42:6, 49:6, 52:10, 60:3. Even Abraham's original call, back when his name was Abram, was to be a blessing to the nations (Genesis 12:1-3).

[d] When we read of Jesus clearing the Temple in Mark, He says, "Is it not written: 'My house will be called a house of prayer for all nations'? But you have turned it into a den of robbers." (Mark 11:17) He is standing in the Court of Gentiles, which is the only part of the Temple that non-Jews could go. They erected a 3-cubit barrier (about 4.5 feet) and posted signs threatening death to any non-Jew who crossed. Before Jesus shut it down, this market had taken over the only place Gentiles could worship.

Who does Jesus say is their father? How does He support this claim?

If they were truly children of Abraham, they would believe like Abraham did. If they were truly children of God, they would receive the one sent by God (Jesus). He calls them children of the devil because, like the devil, they are murderers and liars. Jesus didn't credit them based on who their biological parents were. And your biological story doesn't affect your standing with Him either! According to Jesus, our actions, not our lineage, reveal our spiritual father.

What do your actions reveal? Who would Jesus call your father?

God's Story in Your Life

It's hard to see hints God is dropping along the way toward an event you don't yet know. Instead, let's look at your past and see how God worked in your life, even when you didn't yet see. Think about a "twist" in your past. You may have suddenly lost your job, been in a car accident, or experienced the death of a loved one. Now look at the months leading up to that event.

How did God prepare you for that trial before it happened?

God taught me a lot about Himself in 2017, when my parents both died in unrelated accidents just 13 days apart.[a] But he was working in my life long before the accidents. He built my faith in little ways that helped me trust Him in this painful season. He also aligned my finances to make it possible to take unpaid leave for over a month.

From a young age, my parents encouraged us to memorize scripture through programs like Awana. In the months after their deaths, I rarely even opened a Bible. The Holy Spirit reminded me of those verses when I needed them most. Through other events in my past, I learned the empathy that helped me forgive Jack before I even knew his name.

All of this and much, much more is the faithfulness of God to prepare me before the "twist" ever came. He is working in your life right now, even if you don't know or see it yet.

Journal a prayer of gratitude for God's faithfulness in life's twists.

---

[a] If you want to know more about my story, you can check out my blog. I recommend starting with the post Confused but Confident, which I wrote the day my mother died. imperfectprogresstitles.com/2017/04/12/confused-but-confident/

Daily Tracking Sheet ___ / ___ / ___

Today's writing goal is _____, which I will celebrate by _____.

I will connect with _____, by _____.

I will move my body by _____.

Today's Personal Goals:

1:

2:

3:

Reflection Questions

Today's Biggest Victory:

Today's Biggest Challenge and How I Overcame:

I am grateful for:

1:
2:
3:

Day 14: Take a Deep Breath

Jesus said to them, "Truly, truly, I say to you, before Abraham was, I am." John 8:58

Writing Your Story

Real talk. As I write this, I am significantly behind. For this year's NaNoWriMo, I set up two profiles, one to write this Bible Study, and the other tied to a young adult (YA) fantasy novel. Initially, I crushed it! On day 7, however, I missed writing in my YA story. On day 8, I was sick and struggled through writing two paragraphs. Not until day 13 did I make progress on this project (and the YA still sits forlornly abandoned). That's an entire week of doing little to nothing!

Meanwhile, I kept seeing everyone's word counts climb on Facebook and Twitter. The further I fell behind, the harder it was to get motivated to start again. Imposter Syndrome hit **hard**, making me doubt myself for attempting to write this study. Fortunately, you are reading this. That means I finished!

We are almost halfway through this journey. Every day you have attacked the story and done your best. Or maybe you haven't. Perhaps you already hit your word count goal for the entire month, or maybe you haven't even reached 10%. Whatever the case, use today to catch up, explore other creative ideas, or even take a break and write nothing at all.

John's Story   Read John 8:48-59

What stands out most to you from John 8:48-59?

Venture with me back to the book of Exodus, where the Hebrews are in slavery for four hundred years. God appoints a baby, a basket, and a princess to prepare his main man, Moses. But Moses takes things into his own hands, kills an Egyptian, and runs off for 40 years. God isn't done with Moses and lights a bush on fire to get his attention. He tells Moses, "You are my man. Go set my people free." They go back and forth a bit, and then we get to Exodus 3:13, where Moses asks God who he should say sent him.[a]

God said to Moses, "I am who I am." And he said, "Say this to the people of Israel: 'I am has sent me to you.'"[b]

"I am" (YHWH), spoken in Hebrew, sounds like "Yahweh" ("Jehovah" once Latinized). This verse in Exodus 3 is not the first time YHWH is found in the Bible. But scholars believe Moses wrote the first five books of the Bible (the Torah) later in his life, after God introduced Himself here in Exodus 3.

This became the primary name for God. YHWH is so sacred to Jews that, even today, they will not write it on anything that may be destroyed or mishandled.[17] This is the name used for God throughout the Old Testament, showing up 1,606 times in the Torah alone and over 6,800 times in the Old Testament.[18]

Why would God choose "I AM" as His name? What does it imply?

---

[a] Don't like my summary? Go check out Exodus 1-3 for yourself.
[b] Exodus 3:14

By calling Himself "I AM," God asserts His self-existence. He wasn't created; He's not dependent on anyone or anything for His power and authority. He is God simply because He is God. Thus, He introduces Himself as, "I am that I am."

This statement declares His aseity (self-existence), which is your SAT word of the day.[19] The aseity of God is foundational to our faith.

Why does God's aseity (self-existence) matter? How does it affect us that God is self-existent?

Here are three ways God's aseity affects us daily:[20]
- **Grace can be free.** Because God is self-existent, He has no needs and can give to us freely. Grace as a free gift is the foundation of the gospel and what makes Christianity unique.
- **We learn to give freely.** Having a God who needs nothing from us, we serve others as we have been served by God.
- **God is glorified.** Because God has no needs, His glory is magnified. A god created or sustained by an external source cannot be God.

How does God's aseity change the way you live?

We have spent a considerable amount of time talking about the "seven signs" (seven miracles) in John. John also uses another set of seven to display the divinity of Jesus: the seven "I AM"s.

What are the seven I AM statements Jesus uses in the Gospel of John?[a]

6:35	
8:12	
10:7	
10:11,14	
11:25	
14:6	
15:1	

[a] John 7:37 always makes me think Jesus called Himself the Living Water. He calls Himself living water, but it is not an "I AM" statement. He also doesn't use an I AM statement with the Woman at the Well. Thus, Living Water didn't make the list, creating the perfect trick question to stump Bible nerds!

Which "I AM" statement resonates most with you? Why?

God's Story in Your Life

Your purpose matters. But your purpose is not about you. Remember that ultimately it is God who works and wills according to His purpose.[a]

If you are feeling overwhelmed and burdened by the purpose God has given you, check your perspective. Are you trying to do this for God, or are you cooperating with God and working according to His design?

How can you rest in God today?

God's desire to partner with us can be confusing. This is even more true considering our smallness beside His power, wisdom, authority, and resources. Why would He want to partner with me? What do I contribute to this relationship?

The best way I can wrap my mind around it is to think about making cookies. If you have ever made cookies with a child, you know it is messier, takes longer, and is less perfect than following the same recipe alone in your clean kitchen.

So why bother going through all that hassle, when the same or better cookies come from working alone? I never ask a child to bake cookies with me because I need her help. It's because I want to spend time with her and create memories baking together.

God wants me to be a part of what He is doing. He could zap a book into print and distribute it without my help! Instead, He gets His kitchen covered in flour because He wants to share the process with me. He knows where I fall short, but He is patient with me because He loves me.

And He loves you too. The weight of your purpose isn't on your shoulders! He is the one doing the heavy lifting. And He always lets us lick the spoon.

---

[a] Philippians 2:13 and Romans 8:26-28

Daily Tracking Sheet   __ / __ / __

Today's writing goal is _____, which I will celebrate by _____.

I will connect with _____, by _____.

I will move my body by _____.

Today's Personal Goals:

1:

2:

3:

Reflection Questions

Today's Biggest Victory:

Today's Biggest Challenge and How I Overcame:

I am grateful for:

1:
2:
3:

Day 15: Midpoint–Raise the Stakes

Jesus said to them, "If you were blind, you would have no guilt; but now that you say, 'We see,' your guilt remains. John 9:41

Writing Your Story

Look at you! Here we are on day 15 and you are still showing up! Every time we set out to do what God has called us to do there can be resistance. I am so proud of you for continuing to do the work. Don't stress if you haven't finished your Fun and Games; we are not writing our Midpoint today.

Although the Midpoint is a single scene, we are going to take two days to talk about it because it's so important. A good Midpoint is the difference between stories propelled into the second half with momentum and those with a "soggy middle" that limp to the Climax. Today and tomorrow, we will discuss how to craft a rock-solid Midpoint to kick-start your second half.

According to the BS2, your Midpoint should contain three elements: a raise-the-stakes event, a False Victory or False Defeat, and the intersection of A Story and B Story. Today we are going to break down four ways to raise the stakes with your Midpoint. You can use any combination of these approaches. You want to make moving backward hard or nearly impossible. Like the Catalyst you used to push your protagonist into Act 2, your Midpoint will propel them into the second half.

Love Story Shift

Take the love story to the next level with a first kiss, a proposal, marriage, or some other relationship milestone. After fourteen years of hard labor, Jacob married Rebecca, shifting the story in a new direction.

Pro tip: don't share a husband with your sister! The desire for Jacob's affection causes a rivalry between Rebecca and Leah, which lasts until Rebecca dies. Now that Jacob has found a wife, he shifts his focus to gathering cattle and getting ready for the unavoidable encounter with Esau.

What relationship shift could raise the stakes in your story?

Time clocks and deadlines.

While it can be cliché, there is a reason so many books and movies have a "ticking clock" in the second half. Setting a deadline or starting a countdown refocuses both the characters and the audience. Suddenly, there is only so much time left before it is too late. But don't just introduce a ticking clock; that clock needs to matter to the story.

Here are three ways to make sure your ticking clock raises the stakes:[21]

- **Maintain tension through to the deadline.** If your ticking clock is a school dance, there needs to be steady pressure on your protagonist to find a date.
- **Increase obstacles as the deadline nears.** As the clock counts down, the difficulty ramps up. The longer they wait to find a date for the dance, the more girls are unavailable.
- Unless you are deconstructing the ticking clock trope, **make sure your hero takes the clock seriously.** If your protagonist is fine attending the dance without a date, the ticking clock isn't useful.

How could a ticking clock raise the stakes in your story?

Plot Twist!

There are hundreds of ways you can include a twist in your story to keep the reader guessing. Most stories have more than one twist, but typically, the biggest twist happens at the Midpoint.

There is no way to cover every plot twist in this lesson. If you are looking for ideas, there are several substantial lists out there to help spark your imagination.[22]

It's not enough to twist the plot just to surprise your readers, without setup and payoff. Let's look at three important ingredients for a plot twist to work in your story.[23]

- **Plausibility**: The plot twist should fit the rules you constructed. Violating established world-building destroys your reader's trust. This will break their immersion and decrease their investment in the story. That's the opposite of your goal!
- **Foreshadowing**: Plot twists that land with readers have set up. They are a surprise grown out of seeds sown along the way.[a]
- **Surprise**: If the reader sees it coming, it isn't a twist. Yes, it should have foreshadowing and fit into the rules of your world, but it shouldn't be something they see coming on the first read.[b]

What game-changing plot twist could raise the stakes in your story?

Get Everyone Together

Just because you write a big party doesn't mean you are raising the stakes. For this to work, you need more than an event that pulls everyone together. Here are a few ways you can use a gathering to raise the stakes:

- **"Out" your protagonist as a part of the Act 2 world**. The event can convince your protagonist that they have a place in this new world. Or it could show others they are no longer an outsider.
- **Prove how much your protagonist has changed**. Create a scenario for your protagonist that resembles an event prior to the Catalyst. But, this time, they respond differently, highlighting how much they have changed.[c]
- **Bring Act 1 and Act 2 worlds together**. Their parents, ex-boyfriend, or some other person from their old life shows up to the event and sees them in this new environment.

How can you use a party, celebration, or other gathering to raise the stakes in your story?

There is no limit to how these four ways to raise the stakes can be mixed and matched in your Midpoint. Have fun with your story. For example, the first four *Harry Potter* books all use the Halloween celebration (event) at their Midpoint. But they also each include another way to raise the stakes.

---

[a] Don't feel you need to go back and fix the first half of your story to include more foreshadowing. Focus on finishing the story before getting distracted editing and rewriting.

[b] As stated in day 13, the "surprise" should be proportional to your intended audience. *The Magic Treehouse*, was written for 1st through 4th graders. The twists in this series are easy to predict, but it doesn't make it bad writing.

[c] Your main character has not yet learned the theme and fixed their fatal flaw. Their change at this point in the story should be mostly external, not the internal / character change that will come later.

John's Story

Read John 9

What stands out most to you from John 9?

How is this different from Jesus' other miracles?

In other Gospels, we see Jesus heal the blind, but only in John does He do it in such a dramatic way. First, He makes mud with His own spit and slathers it on the man's eyes, which is pretty gross. Then He sends him away, instructing him to find the pool of Siloam, seeming to disregard the challenge this poses a blind man.

This miracle leaves the Pharisees divided. Some point out that He is (yet again) breaking the Sabbath, while others question how anyone not sent by God could perform such signs. They repeatedly ask for an explanation, both from the man and from his parents, desperate to prove Jesus is in the wrong.

What point is Jesus making about the Pharisees in verse 41?

Jesus calls them out for their willful blindness. We all have our own pet sins. Unfortunately, the Bible doesn't give any of us an asterisk. The Bible does not say, "You shall not lie, except Jenn can lie on her taxes." To willfully live in sin is to choose blindness over the truth of God's Word.

How have you been willfully "blind"? What truth do you try not to see?

God's Story in Your Life

When we are on the path God has put before us, we will encounter moments that take our commitment to the next level. This doesn't have to be a negative; it can be a moment to re-commit to pursuing the purpose God has given you. Consider the four ways we discussed raising the stakes in our books and apply them to your purpose:

- What would it mean to make a shift in your relationship with God?
- How can you use a time limit to refocus your effort on your purpose?
- What change in direction may be necessary for you to keep making progress?
- How can you gather everyone involved? How could this help renew your commitment to the cause?

What one thing will you do this week to "raise the stakes" in the purpose God has given you?

Daily Tracking Sheet

___ / ___ / ___

Today's writing goal is _____, which I will celebrate by _____.

I will connect with _____, by _____.

I will move my body by _____.

Today's Personal Goals:

1:

2:

3:

Reflection Questions

Today's Biggest Victory:

Today's Biggest Challenge and How I Overcame:

I am grateful for:
1:
2:
3:

Week 3 Discussion and Review

Assemble the people, men, women, and little ones, and the sojourner within your towns, that they may hear and learn to fear the Lord your God, and be careful to do all the words of this law, Deuteronomy 31:12

Story Check-In

How is writing going?

What has gone well? What one sentence are you most proud of or want to share?

Where did you get stuck or where do you need feedback?

Bible Study Check-In

What most surprised you from John 7-9?

How have you been willfully "blind"? What biblical truth do you avoid or deny?

Read and discuss this story of the woman caught in adultery found in John 7:53-8:11.[a]

God's Story in Your Life

What works best for you to avoid burnout? How did you rest in God this week?

What will you do this week to "raise the stakes" in your pursuit of purpose?

Pray and Close

Thank God for how he has prepared you for twists in the past.

Pray for renewed commitment to your purpose as you go into the second half of this study.

My notes and doodles:

---

[a] John 7:53-8:11 is not in the original manuscripts. The most recent manuscripts to include this passage are from AD 500. Most scholars believe this is probably a true story and John might have recorded it. But they also don't think it belongs here. The passages before and after both take place on the same day, in the same place, and flow together like a continuous scene. My decision to skip it is not discounting its truth. I skipped it because we are looking at John's story structure and scholars do not agree this belongs where it is in John's story.

Day 16: Midpoint

"For this reason the Father loves me, because I lay down my life that I may take it up again." John 10:17

Writing Your Story

We have passed the half-way point! Congratulations! It's easy to get caught up in how our word count compares to others. Don't fall into that trap! Thousands of people "win" NaNoWriMo every year with 50,000 words and then publish nothing! No one cares if your book takes you a month to write or three years.[a] Don't let the Devil distract you from finishing your book. He enjoys it when we waste time and energy comparing our progress to an arbitrary standard.

Today, we continue our discussion on using your Midpoint to propel your story into the second half. Remember, the three elements of a successful Midpoint are raising the stakes, a False Victory or False Defeat, and intersecting A Story and B Story. Yesterday we considered how to raise the stakes. Now let's discuss the other two elements and explore how to bring it all together.

False Victory or False Defeat

On Day 12, you determined the trajectory of your Fun and Games. Stories with "Onward and Upward" first halves frequently use a False Victory at the Midpoint. Meanwhile, "Floundering Forward" stories usually pivot with a False Defeat. In both cases, the idea is to shift the story's direction. Remember, your Midpoint needs to pull your protagonist from the first half of your story and force them into the second half. Like your Catalyst, the Midpoint should push them hard enough there is no turning back.

In a False Victory, the protagonist should get what they wanted. They won! Here we are. But wait, the story is only halfway over! Besides, they still need to learn their lesson.

Here are some approaches to writing a False Victory:
- He gets what he wanted… but it doesn't make him happy.
- She gets part of what she wanted or makes progress toward her goal.
- They get what they wanted… and it's immediately taken away.
- He gets what he wants… but learns it is a counterfeit.
- She gets what she wants… but it costs more than she expected.

The key to writing a False Defeat is making the protagonist believe they failed completely. Though the defeat must be substantial, it can't be the dark-night-of-the-soul level defeat (that's nearer to the Climax).

Here are some ideas for crafting a False Defeat:
- They fail a deadline, making success seem impossible.
- He is rejected in a way that feels final.
- She breaks or loses what she thought she needed.
- The enemy makes major progress.
- A new obstacle appears that wasn't in play before.

What type of False Victory or False Defeat works for your Midpoint?

---

[a] *The Night Circus*, the most famous "NaNo Novel" on many of the lists I found, was written over three NaNoWriMo's. That's 3 years!

Merging A Story and B Story

We keep coming back to the idea your character's inner journey (B Story) should drive the outer events (A Story). But that's all been invisible to our protagonist. He doesn't realize he needs to learn the power of friendship. She doesn't understand that she has a spending problem and cannot possibly earn enough money to dig out of the hole. They don't understand that this budding romance is doomed if they don't learn to communicate.

Now it's time for the A Story plot to intersect with the B Story theme. Before you go too far, remember that your hero is not learning their lesson and fixing their internal flaw. We still have the second half of the book. But it is time for them to see that their flaw is keeping them from succeeding or finding happiness in that success.

Often, this intersection of A Story and B Story causes one or more B Story character(s) to enter the A Story plotline. Maybe the love interest joins the questing party, or the mentor figure meets the rest of the chess team. This is a way to signal to your reader that the two stories are intersecting.

How can your A Story and B Story intersect? What B Story character can join your A Story?

Bringing it all together.

Now you have all three components: Raise the Stakes, False Victory or False Defeat, and merging A Story with B Story. But how do you fit all three into a single scene? What holds these three pieces together?

Although there are many alternatives, using your theme as the glue is often the most effective approach to crafting your Midpoint. Root the other two components of your Midpoint in the bringing together of your A Story and B Story.

Let the pressure from your protagonist's fear or internal flaw put in motion the raise-the-stakes event you chose yesterday.

For example, his fear of commitment could convince her he isn't serious, causing her to choose a college in Arkansas (ticking clock). Three chapters ago, the protagonist chose a shortcut to avoid addressing their inner flaw. But that "shortcut" led the group into a trap set by the enemy (plot twist).

How can your B Story trigger the way you raise the stakes?

Think about your False Victory or False Defeat. The reason this victory isn't genuine should relate to the life lesson the protagonist needs to learn. Their defeat should come from steps they took to avoid facing their fear. So far, the protagonist has worked toward their goal while avoiding their fear and shirking responsibility. And that's why they're failing.

How can your protagonist's fear or internal flaw cause the False Victory or False Defeat?

John's Story Read John 10:1-21

What stands out to you most from John 10:1-21?

Why does John use this as his Midpoint? How is this a turning point in the Gospel?

John's B Story is about believing in Jesus. How does that factor into this scene?

Today's reading is a continuation of the scene we began yesterday when Jesus healed the blind man.[a] This scene, with the healing discussed yesterday and the teaching from today, serves as the Midpoint of the book of John. It began with a healing from Jesus unlike any of His previous miracles.[b] There is a shift that comes after this scene. Jesus will focus the rest of his ministry on the disciples.

God's Story in Your life

Where have you encountered a False Victory or a False Defeat?

How did your internal flaw cause that False Victory or False Defeat?

How can you attack your internal flaw by increasing your commitment to your purpose?

My first NaNoWriMo, I crushed the 50k word count goal, with more than 140k! But when it ended, my story was a chaotic mess. I spent most of the next year trying to edit it into something salvageable. This "False Victory" came from my fear of not being enough. I was so focused on proving I was enough, I prioritized the word count over a cohesive story. Ultimately, I had to scrap most of what I wrote and start over.

---

[a] We know this is still part of the same scene because in verse 21 the onlookers are talking about the miracle He just performed.
[b] Until now, Jesus' has used His words for every miracle (in John). In this miracle, He is hands-on in a way that grabs our attention. He spat in the dirt, made mud, and spread it on the man's eyes! This is a sharp contrast from the other miracles John recorded.

Daily Tracking Sheet   ___ / ___ / ___

Today's writing goal is _____, which I will celebrate by _____.

I will connect with _____, by _____.

I will move my body by _____.

Today's Personal Goals:

1:

2:

3:

Reflection Questions

Today's Biggest Victory:

Today's Biggest Challenge and How I Overcame:

I am grateful for:
1:
2:
3:

Day 17: Bad Guys Close In–The "Bad Guys"

The Jews picked up stones again to stone him. John 10:31

Writing Your Story

Congratulations on finishing your Midpoint! We are now in the second half and racing toward the Finale. The Bad Guys Close In uses a similar structure to the Fun and Games.

You still keep promises, create momentum, and maintain tension. What we discussed about trajectory is still true, although most stories are on the opposite path from the Fun and Games (because of the Midpoint twist). There is still foreshadowing what is to come, except now we are preparing readers for the twists and turns at the end of the story.

We find the biggest difference in the B Story. In the Fun and Games, we wanted the B Story to run parallel to the A Story. We used the Midpoint to intersect the two. Throughout the Bad Guys Close In, they will become more and more entwined as we move toward the Finale. We characterize this mingling of A Story and B Story with the two types of "bad guys" that are closing in.

Internal and external bad guys.

The external bad guys oppose your protagonist's A Story. If you are writing a spy thriller, the external bad guys would be the enemy agents. Don't let the term "guys" confuse you; sometimes it's a dragon, a patch of cactus, or a broken cell phone. Ultimately, the external bad guys are the people and obstacles that keep your characters from their goal.

Who or what are the external bad guys in your story?

The bad guys that are most important are not on the outside, threatening to tear your protagonist limb from limb. What matters most to your story are the internal bad guys, AKA the internal flaw that your character still hasn't overcome. This flaw has always been there, but now it's "closing in" or becoming a real problem for your protagonist by impeding what they are trying to accomplish.

In your Midpoint, your protagonist recognized for the first time how much this flaw was holding them back. Now that realization should play out more explicitly over these next several scenes. The protagonist must experience how much their fear, and reluctance to learn their lesson, is creating pain in their life.

How are the internal bad guys preventing your protagonist from reaching their goal?

Keeping promises as bad guys close in.

But what scenes belong in the Bad Guys Close In? More of the same promise-keeping scenes as you wrote in the Fun and Games except for one major difference: the Bad Guys are closing in!

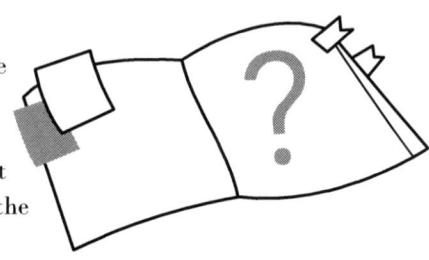

Continue thinking through all those fun scenes and ideas that made you want to write this story. But use each scene to show the internal or external bad guys (ideally both) getting in the way.

What are 2-3 scenes you still need to include to keep your "promise of the premise?"

1.

2.

3.

How can your internal and external bad guys show up in each scene?

1.

2.

3.

## John's Story					Read John 10:22-42

What stands out most to you from John 10:22-42?

How do the internal and external bad guys show up in today's reading?

The external "bad guys" in John are the religious leaders who work to discredit or remove Jesus because He threatens their power. In today's reading, they try to stone Him! John's internal "bad guys" refers to anything hindering people from believing in Jesus.

How does Jesus combat unbelief in this chapter? Is it effective?

Do your works reflect you are a child of God?

God's Story in Your Life

What external bad guys oppose your purpose? How have these "closed in?"

What internal bad guys oppose your purpose? How have these "closed in?"

How can you avoid being derailed by your external and internal bad guys?

Daily Tracking Sheet ___ / ___ / ___

Today's writing goal is _____, which I will celebrate by _____.

I will connect with _____, by _____.

I will move my body by _____.

Today's Personal Goals:

1:

2:

3:

Reflection Questions

Today's Biggest Victory:

Today's Biggest Challenge and How I Overcame:

I am grateful for:

1:
2:
3:

Day 18: Bad Guys Close In—Beginning at the End

Martha said to him, "I know that he will rise again in the resurrection on the last day." Jesus said to her, "I am the resurrection and the life. Whoever believes in me, though he die, yet shall he live," John 11:24-25

Writing Your Story

Welcome to day 2 of looking at the Bad Guys Close In. Before we can outline the structure and trajectory, we need to know the broad strokes of your Finale, so you can drive your story toward that picture. I'm not telling you to jump to day 26 of this study, but we are going to spend a little time today thinking about how you want your story to end.

Beginning at the end.

Does he get the girl? Does she slay the dragon? Do they stop the Dark Lord? Does he solve the mystery? Does she reconcile with her mother? What about the B Story: Does he learn to forgive? Does she overcome her anger issue? Do they discover the danger of lies? Does he become more responsible? Does she quit letting people walk all over her? You don't need to know the details of the ending, but it is helpful to have a clear idea of where you are going.

How do you want your A Story to end?

How do you want your B Story to end?

	A Story Success	**A Story Failure**
B Story Success	**The Happily Ever After:** they learn their lesson and thus succeed in their goal. Example: *Redeeming Love*	**The Lesson of Failure:** they learn their lesson despite failing their quest or goal. Example: *Fahrenheit 451*
B Story Failure	**The Bittersweet Victory:** they succeed in their goal but don't learn their lesson. Example: *Gone with the Wind*	**The Villain Origin Story:** they don't learn their lesson and thus fail their quest (or fail the quest and thus don't learn their lesson). Example: *Heartless*

Now that you know where your A Story is going, what must happen for them to reach that point? For example, stories where the hero ultimately fails often show them close to success at the end of the Fun and Games. Success is in sight, just in time for everything to go wrong!

The ending also affects the journey, which we will discuss more tomorrow. Think about Scarlet in *Gone with the Wind* compared to Angel in *Redeeming Love*. Angel makes progress toward accepting and giving love while Scarlett digs in her heels, refusing to change.

Where does your story fit in the above table?

How does this impact your Bad Guys Close In?

78 | Day 18

Foreshadowing twists and turns.

Besides the constant small twists and turns of any story, there are two major twist opportunities we need to prepare the reader for. These are the All is Lost (day 22) and the High Tower Surprise (day 27).

You don't need to know your exact plan for either scene right now. But if you have an idea, it will help with foreshadowing.

- Will there be a betrayal by someone in the group?
- Will the magic behave in a new or unexpected way?
- Will a new danger come into play?
- Will an antagonist appear who claims to have been pulling strings from behind the scenes all along?

A good twist is delightfully entertaining, while a poorly handled one can rob readers of satisfaction and destroy immersion. Unless you are writing for Early Readers or Middle Grade, you probably don't want to reveal the twist explicitly and spoil the surprise. But twists also shouldn't come out of nowhere, or readers can feel cheated. Ideally, we want our readers to think, "Why didn't I see that coming?" instead of, "How did that happen?"

What foreshadowing needs to be woven into your Bad Guys Close In?

John's Story   Read John 11:1-46

What stands out most to you from John 11:1-46?

Jesus operates throughout the book of John with the clarity of someone who has already heard the end of the story and is watching it unfold. Never is this clearer than in the way Jesus speaks and reacts at the start of this chapter. John highlights this foreknowledge by contrasting Jesus' response with the people around Him. We see this right away when he says in verse 4 that Lazarus' illness does not lead to death.

This seems inconsistent if we think Jesus is saying, "Lazarus will not die." But that is not what He says. Instead, He says this illness (this story) will not end in death. That's not where the story is going. Instead, "It is for the glory of God, so that the Son of God may be glorified."

Aside from the resurrection, this is probably the most important miracle John records. We have the benefit of hindsight. Take some time to consider this situation from the perspectives of those present.

What do these verses tell us about the crowd's perspective?   v19,31,36,37,41,45-46

What do these verses tell us about the disciples' perspective?   v8,12-13,16

How do the disciples display faith despite not knowing the ending?   v16

Bad Guys Close In | 79

What do these verses tell us about Mary's perspective?   v3,20,29,32

What do these verses tell us about Martha's perspective?   v3,20-21,22,24,27-28,39

How does Jesus encourage each sister uniquely?   v23-26,33-35

This is my favorite part! Mary is more of an empath, while Martha is very logical. Jesus meets both with equal compassion, but His interaction is unique to their personalities. With Martha, He discusses the theology of resurrection, but He takes time to cry with Mary. God loves us all equally, but He also loves us uniquely.

How does each sister display faith despite not knowing the ending?

How can you act in faith when you don't understand where the story is going?

God's Story in Your Life

Unfortunately, short of divine inspiration, there isn't a way for you to get a sneak peek at where your story ends. (Honestly, we would probably give up if God gave us the entire plan from day one.) However, now that we are about halfway through this study, this is a fantastic time to reexamine how you **want** your story to end.

How has your understanding of your A Story (your purpose) shifted since day 1?

What is one thing you can do today to help push the story in the right direction?

Daily Tracking Sheet ___ / ___ / ___

Today's writing goal is _____, which I will celebrate by _____.

I will connect with _____, by _____.

I will move my body by _____.

Today's Personal Goals:

1:

2:

3:

Reflection Questions

Today's Biggest Victory:

Today's Biggest Challenge and How I Overcame:

I am grateful for:

1:
2:
3:

Day 19: Bad Guys Close In–Bouncing A and B Story

So the chief priests made plans to put Lazarus to death as well, because on account of him many of the Jews were going away and believing in Jesus. John 12:10-11

Writing Your Story

Yesterday, we identified the general shape of your Bad Guys Close In and considered what foreshadowing you may need for the twists and turns to come. Today we want to revisit the "bouncing ball" concept from Day 10. That same progress, obstacle, progress, obstacle momentum should carry through the entire story, and the Bad Guys Close In is no different. What changes in this beat is why the ball is bouncing: we want those bounces to be driven by our B Story.

Identify the bounces.

Let's start with a list of all the scenes you need to get your characters into place for the climactic ending to your story. This table should look familiar. Write out the scenes you know you need and then fill in any gaps to maintain the bouncing structure we've been working with since Day 10. *(Ignore B Story for now.)*

A Story Progress	B Story	A Story Obstacle	B Story

Winning B Story. *"Happily Ever After" or "Lesson of Failure" endings*

It's tougher for me to guide you in this part of the plot, because it's crucial that you're led by the "shape" of your individual story. That said, if you are heading towards an ending where the hero learns their lesson, each bounce should trigger accordingly. This means they make progress when the hero's choices align with the lesson they are learning. Similarly, their failure to act on the lesson causes or exacerbates the obstacles.

If you are writing a winning B Story, use the "B Story" columns to consider:

- How is this progress caused by your protagonist facing their fear or learning their lesson?
- How is this obstacle caused (or made worse) by your protagonist's internal flaw?
- Not every A Story event has a B Story trigger. But the more you use the B Story to trigger A Story bounces, the more your story will resonate with its theme.

Failing B Story. *"Bittersweet Victory" or "Villain Origin Story" endings*

But what if you are Marissa Meyer writing *Heartless* or Margaret Mitchell writing *Gone with the Wind*? How do these bounces push you toward an ending where the hero doesn't learn their lesson?

Obstacles work much the same as in the successful B Story tales we discussed above. But in these stories, the hero makes progress by pushing against learning their lesson. They keep beating away their fatal flaw, even as it comes closer and closer.

Think about Scarlett in *Gone with the Wind*. She never entertains the idea she doesn't love Ashley or recognizes the potential for love in her marriage to Rhett. Each time she feels threatened, she takes control and does what she thinks will make her happy. As time passes, her flaw becomes more apparent, and Rhett eventually leaves her, alone and unhappy, to live the life she thought she wanted.

If you are writing a Failing B Story, use the "B Story" columns to consider:

- How is this obstacle caused (or made worse) by your protagonist's internal flaw?
- How does the protagonist push against learning their lesson to make this progress?
- Not every A Story event has a B Story trigger. But the more you use the B Story to trigger A Story bounces, the more your story will resonate with its theme.

Remember, these are broad generalizations. You could write the Bad Guys Close In as if it's leading to a happy ending, then surprise readers by having the hero reject the lesson at the last moment. For every plotting "rule," there is at least one novel that broke it and still became a success.

John's Story **Read John 11:45-12:11**

What stands out most to you from John 11:45-12:11?

Sacrificing belief for personal gain. John 11:45-57, 12:9-11

How does B Story progress in this section? How does that trigger progress in A Story?

Jesus is closing in on the cross (A Story), and people are believing in Him (B Story). As more people believe in Jesus, the religious leaders become increasingly desperate to stop Him. Thus, we see the B Story of people believing in Him becoming the driving force of the A Story.

Someone just rose from the dead! Seeing such an undeniable sign, it's reasonable to expect everyone to believe in Jesus. But the religious leaders push against belief. Fearing the Romans will take away their power if too many people believe in Jesus, they reject the signs in front of them. They plot to get Jesus—and now Lazarus—out of the way because their desire for power outweighs their need for truth.

How have your desires blinded you from, or caused you to reject, a truth God is revealing?

Sacrificing personal gain for belief. John 12:1-8

How does B Story progress in this section? How does that trigger progress in A Story?

How do Mary and Martha serve Jesus from their unique personalities?

How willing are you to sacrifice for what you believe?

Writing Your Story with God

Sometimes we can be guilty of getting so caught up in what we are doing in pursuit of our purpose that we miss the way God wants to work within us. Today, let's take a step back and consider how our personal B Stories are going.

What will you do today to work on the life lesson God is teaching you?

Daily Tracking Sheet

__ / __ / __

Today's writing goal is _____, which I will celebrate by _____.

I will connect with _____, by _____.

I will move my body by _____.

Today's Personal Goals:

1:

2:

3:

Reflection Questions

Today's Biggest Victory:

Today's Biggest Challenge and How I Overcame:

I am grateful for:
1:
2:
3:

Day 20: Bad Guys Close In–Tension and Momentum

Nevertheless, many even of the authorities believed in him, but for fear of the Pharisees they did not confess it, so that they would not be put out of the synagogue; for they loved the glory that comes from man more than the glory that comes from God. John 12:42-43

Writing Your Story

Just like our Fun and Games, it isn't enough for the ball to bounce up and down in place. The Bad Guys Close In needs to have a feeling of momentum. The bad guys, both internal and external, need to become a bigger and bigger threat as we march toward the All is Lost.

Raising the threat level.

To make this believable, the threat needs to be increasing each time there is an encounter with the bad guys in this story. If your questing party is venturing to the lair of the Dark Lord, their first encounter with his minions may be a single scouting party. Then the next is a battalion of light troops, then an entire calvary division, and eventually a full force attacking army. Each encounter is a bigger threat because they are closer and closer to reaching the Dark Lord's lair.

How can you escalate the A Story threat level?

Increased consequences from their internal flaw.

The B Story threat should rise in tension at the same rate. Your hero who needs to learn the power of friendship should feel more and more consequences each time he doesn't trust his fellow adventurers. Perhaps the first time, it's just a lost map or them getting off the trail. Maybe the next time it's poison ivy or a dead end that sends them back to walk around the other way. Eventually, his distrust may cause someone's death.

How can you escalate the B Story consequences?

Higher cost of progress.

While the threats and consequences are increasing, it should also become more difficult to make progress.

In our A Story, this plays out as needing to take bigger risks or make bigger moves to progress against the enemy forces. Bigger gestures of love are required to escalate the relationship. The team only makes progress by conquering bigger traps or obstacles.

How is the price of A Story progress escalating?

Similarly, B Story progress requires bigger proof the hero is learning their lesson. Initially, it was letting the guy who studied maps of this area for years guide the group. Then letting the former general decide how to fight against the growing minion forces. But the price of learning to trust needs to get higher. Maybe it's having the faith to let the strongest man in the group throw them across a ravine full of deadly snakes.

How is the price of B Story progress escalating?

A great example of this escalation is the story of Gideon. Initially, God asks him to do a small thing (gather meat and bread) and gives him a small sign (lighting it on fire). Then God asks a little more (destroy the altar). God gives him larger signs (the two signs with the fleece) and asks for a larger task (gather an army). Eventually, God tells him to go into battle with only 300 people, and no weapons, after letting him overhear his enemy dreaming about Gideon's victory.[a]

John's Story   Read John 12:12-50

What stands out most to you from John 12:12-50?

How do we see the A Story threat increase (religious leaders closing in on Jesus)?

How do we see the B Story threat increase (fear and unbelief)?

Why are the believing Jews silent (v42-43)?

How is this belief insufficient? (Hint: Matthew 10:32-33)

Today's reading begins with the Triumphal Entry, but by the end, no one will profess Jesus publicly. It's easy to look down on these Jews for their fickle faith. But, ultimately, it's the same fear of man that caused my exuberant worship at youth camp to become silence back at school.

Jesus isn't looking for people who trust Him in secret. The evidence of His divine power is stacking up and so is the pressure from the religious leaders to suppress open support for Him. This forces the Jews who believe to ask themselves how much they will pay for their faith. Unfortunately, John tells us, "For they loved human praise more than praise from God." We must be careful not to make the same mistake.

---

[a] Judges 6:11-7:25

God's Story in Your Life

The more time and effort you put into living out your purpose, the more progress you will make. But this also means you will face more resistance. There is internal resistance, as you tire of the process or lose sight of why you are making sacrifices. Then there is the external resistance from people or organizations who don't want you to succeed. If what you are doing makes an impact for God's kingdom, you will also face spiritual resistance, as the Prince of this World (John 16:11) pushes back against your efforts.

What type of internal, external, and spiritual resistance do you face?

How can you stay focused on your purpose?

While daily habits are powerful, continuing to do the same thing over and over will not keep you moving forward at the same rate.

Think about starting a new exercise program. In the beginning, you will see results because you are moving consistently. Eventually, if the routine doesn't change, you'll experience diminishing returns. But you can increase your workouts because **consistency increases capacity**. As you exercise, your muscles grow used to the strain and your capacity increases.

The same is true in pursuing your purpose. As you make progress, what once had a large impact will provide diminishing returns. There's no need to panic; assess your habits and identify where you can increase your commitment. As you have taken consistent action on your purpose, what was once difficult has become routine.

How has your capacity increased since you started pursuing your purpose?

How can you tweak your habits to keep making progress?

Daily Tracking Sheet ___ / ___ / ___

Today's writing goal is _____, which I will celebrate by _____.

I will connect with _____, by _____.

I will move my body by _____.

Today's Personal Goals:

1:

2:

3:

Reflection Questions

Today's Biggest Victory:

Today's Biggest Challenge and How I Overcame:

I am grateful for:

1:

2:

3:

Week 4 Discussion and Review

And they devoted themselves to the apostles' teaching and the fellowship, to the breaking of bread and the prayers. Acts 2:42

Story Check-In

How is writing going?

What has gone well? What one sentence are you most proud of or want to share?

Where did you get stuck or where do you need feedback?

Bible Study Check-In

What most surprised you from John 10-12?

Why do you think Mary's story is so important to Jesus?

What specific action can you take this week to go "all in" with Jesus?

God's Story in Your Life

What internal, external, and spiritual resistance are you facing?

What can you do to encourage each other to keep going despite these "bad guys"?

Pray and Close

Pray for each other to be strong in faith and willing to pay the "price" of belief.

Pray for strength and increased capacity as you push against internal, external, and spiritual pressures fighting to keep you from your purpose.

My notes and doodles:

Day 21: Bad Guys Close In—Catch Up Day

Then [Jesus] poured water into a basin and began to wash the disciples' feet and to wipe them with the towel that was wrapped around him. John 13:5

Writing Your Story

You made it to the last day of working on the Bad Guys Close In. You are now two-thirds of the way through this study! Congratulations on making it this far. There are no new topics to discuss today; this is an opportunity to rest and catch up on any loose ends before we reach the All is Lost.

When you pour your everything into any creative project, there may be times you feel you have nothing left to give. If that's you, here are the four things I do to get unstuck during NaNoWriMo (or anytime I experience creative burnout):

- **Go to bed**. Take a nap. Give my physical body a break from sitting at a desk and hammering away on a keyboard.
- **Talk it out**. I call my Aunt Patti and talk through my story. Sometimes she asks questions that help me get back on track. Other times, simply talking things out is enough to sort everything out in my head.
- **Pour in inspiration**. Take the time to read a fantasy book, listen to poetry, or visit an art museum. Refill my creative cup that has been pouring out my story.
- **Remember what matters**. It's not about my word count or an arbitrary deadline. It's about writing my story to share it with the world.

What helps you get un-stuck when you experience burnout?

What can you do today to refill your creative juices?

Before you go, note that if your Bad Guys Close In trajectory is Onward and Upward, the last scene of your Bad Guys Close In should be a False Victory. The All is Lost beat is a downward beat, so stories moving upward tend to peak at the end of the Bad Guys Close In. A great example of this is in *Heartless*, where they successfully navigate the maze and are about to make it into Chess. This is the setup for the All Is Lost, when Cathrine will hear her friend screaming through one of the forbidden doors.

John's Story   Read John 13:1-20

What stands out most to you from John 13:1-20?

A mindset for serving (Jesus).   John 13:1-5

Why does John explain all these things Jesus knows? How does it reframe His service?

How can you serve others, even when they are unkind to you?

Accepting service (Peter). John 13:6-10

Why doesn't Peter want Jesus to serve him? How has pride kept you from accepting help?

Why does Peter ask Jesus to bathe him? When have you asked for more than you need?

I am guilty of both mistakes, but especially the second, especially when someone is giving away free things. Something in my mind just flips and I "need" all of it! Before you judge me, think about the last time you took leftovers home after a potluck where all you brought was a bag of chips.

Serving your enemies. John 13:11-20

Every time I read these verses, I am baffled none of the disciples picked up on Judas' betrayal. This is a testament to Jesus' character. Right from the beginning, Jesus knew Judas would eventually betray Him, but He never singles him out or treats him differently. Even here, as He washes the disciples' feet, Jesus does not rush through Judas or, in any other way, single out His betrayer.

How can you serve people who hurt you?

Writing Your Story with God

When we focus too much on the daily "grind" it's easy to lose sight of the bigger picture. Just like it is valuable to take a break when writing, stepping back to remember why you do what you do can help bring your vision back into focus. All the resistance and "bad guys" we have been talking about can steal the joy of doing what God created you to do. Re-centering on your "why" can give you the motivation and inspiration to keep doing the work.

What will you do today to rest and refocus on your purpose?

Who can you reach out to for encouragement (let them serve you)?

Who can you encourage today? How will you serve them?

Daily Tracking Sheet

___ / ___ / ___

Today's writing goal is _____, which I will celebrate by _____.

I will connect with _____, by _____.

I will move my body by _____.

Today's Personal Goals:

1:

2:

3:

Reflection Questions

Today's Biggest Victory:

Today's Biggest Challenge and How I Overcame:

I am grateful for:

1:
2:
3:

Day 22: All Is Lost

Little children, yet a little while I am with you. You will seek me, and just as I said to the Jews, so now I also say to you, 'Where I am going you cannot come.' John 13:33

Writing Your Story

You finished your Bad Guys Close In! Great work! We are two-thirds of the way through our stories and now we are racing toward the Finale. But what came before will effect how this crushing blow comes. Consider these two examples; notice the similarities and differences. (The All Is Lost is in bold.)

> It's been a struggle to get here. Ever since that False Victory in the Midpoint, it's been two steps back for every step forward. Then, **the worst blow yet came out of nowhere and destroyed everything**. But it figures. After all, hasn't everything that could go wrong gone wrong?

> Everything was going so well. Ever since that False Defeat in the Midpoint, it has been onward and upward. Victory was within grasp just moments ago **until the unthinkable happened**. What happens now, with everything in ruins?

How did your Bad Guys Close In end? How does that affect your All Is Lost?

Crushing your hero's spirit.

The All is Lost is not just another bounce of your bouncing ball. This needs to be a decisive blow that will devastate your protagonist's spirit and send them reeling into the Dark Night of the Soul. This should be the worst possible thing that could happen to your protagonist. You want your hero to wonder if there is any way to keep going.

Your All is Lost should attack your protagonist from all sides. We need them so broken they finally make the decision to face their fear and learn their lesson. While you won't use every one of these, here are some aspects to consider as you brainstorm what fits your story.

- How can you **physically** break your protagonist? What injury would make them the most desperate?[a]
- How can you **emotionally** break your protagonist by exploiting their fear, misbelief, or backstory?
- How can you **spiritually** break your protagonist by destroying or proving faulty their faith or hope?
- How can you **isolate** your protagonist to make them feel alone?

How will you "break" your protagonist?

Betrayal.

Betrayal has the benefit of triggering several of these kinds of "breaking." There are two times in the story when betrayal makes the most impact. One is here, in the All is Lost, and the other is in the High Tower Surprise, during the Finale.[b] Since our High Tower Surprise lesson will coincide with two major betrayals in Jesus' life, I have a deeper dive into types of betrayals in the Day 27 study.

---

[a] For example, a singer losing their voice, a dancer needing knee surgery, or a beauty contestant scarring their face.
[b] Betrayal can also work as a Catalyst or Midpoint twist, but that will not be as devastating. There is not enough time for the audience to care about the relationship that is betrayed.

What betrayal could/would make sense at this point in the story?

The Whiff of Death

This is the point of the story where someone or something needs to die. Yes, this is when fantasy authors are famous for killing the mentor figure. But the Whiff of Death doesn't need to be a person dying. It could be someone contemplating suicide, an accident that leaves an individual at death's door, or even a more symbolic death. Perhaps the "love fern" he bought her on their first date dies, mirroring the way their relationship is falling apart.

Whatever you choose, it should mirror the death inside the protagonist. Something is dying, but that death is creating space for the new "Protagonist 2.0" to be born.

How can a "whiff of death" trigger a turning point in your protagonist?

All my fault.

In the Catalyst, something happened to your protagonist, pushing them into the Debate and Break Into 2. The All is Lost is similar, but with a major difference. External circumstances triggered the Catalyst, possibly influenced by the protagonist's fatal flaw. But all the blame for the All is Lost needs to fall on our protagonist; specifically, because they haven't faced their fear or learned their lesson.

How is the All is Lost your protagonist's fault?

How does it prove they haven't learned their lesson yet?

John's Story   Read John 13:21-38

What stands out to you most from John 13:21-38?

Does knowing Satan entered Judas change your understanding of Judas' betrayal?

Prior to Satan entering him, there were signs that Judas wasn't fully committed.[a] It's impossible for us to determine how much of the betrayal was Judas' choices and how much was the influence of Satan.

---
[a] John 12:6 – "…because [Judas] was a thief, and having charge of the moneybag he used to help himself to what was put into it."

After Judas leaves, Jesus shifts His tone. The upcoming chapters contain His last words to the disciples, as he prepares for the cross. He becomes somber and tells them His time to depart is drawing near. The disciples are afraid and confused. They wonder where Jesus is going. Peter, ever the bold one, speaks up, asking Jesus where He is going and why the disciples can't follow.

It's easy to judge Peter with hindsight. But Peter was doing the best he could with the information available to him. He later proves his zeal for Jesus when he cuts off the ear of a soldier.[a] Despite an entire legion of soldiers, Peter will stand to fight, undoubtedly risking his life just like he promised. But when Jesus heals the soldier and goes willingly to be tried and crucified, Peter is confused and afraid. Sometimes it is easier to die for Jesus (one big act of bravery) than it is to live for Him (walking in faith despite uncertainty).

What does "living for Him" look like in your life? Are you willing to pay the daily price?

God's Story in Your Life

Has your spirit ever been crushed? How did you get back up?

What has died in your life?[b] What can grow from this pain?[c]

Sometimes pain in our lives is not our fault but we blame ourselves. Other times it is our fault, and we can learn from the experience. Recognizing the difference is important to our mental health and the ability to keep going after loss.

What have you blamed on yourself that is not your fault?

What pain in your life results from your choices?

What lesson do you need to learn?

---

[a] John 18:10
[b] Remember, this does not need to be the death of a person. It could be giving up on a dream, losing a job, or the death of a friendship/relationship.
[c] Like a seed must die before the plant can bloom, pain can bring new life in the most unexpected ways.

Daily Tracking Sheet ___ / ___ / ___

Today's writing goal is _____, which I will celebrate by _____.

I will connect with _____, by _____.

I will move my body by _____.

Today's Personal Goals:

1:

2:

3:

Reflection Questions

Today's Biggest Victory:

Today's Biggest Challenge and How I Overcame:

I am grateful for:

1:
2:
3:

Day 23: Dark Night of the Soul

But the Helper, the Holy Spirit, whom the Father will send in my name, he will teach you all things and bring to your remembrance all that I have said to you. John 14:26

Writing Your Story

Do you feel the momentum? Congratulations on making it to Day 23! We are almost there. If you need a moment to catch your breath, that's ok. Today our protagonists are also taking a break to handle whatever awful things we cooked up in the All is Lost.

Another Debate

The Dark Night of the Soul is like the Debate in Act 1, giving your character a chance to process what happened in the All Is Lost. This also allows the reader to feel the hurt with the protagonist and to empathize with their struggle. They may experience depression, but it could also be other emotions, like anger or thirst for revenge. Trust the character you have created; stay consistent with how they would react to the All Is Lost.

Not every story has time for multiple scenes here. Katniss in the *Hunger Games* doesn't have time for a multi-scene Dark Night of the Soul because there are other child soldiers out there, trying to kill her. She spends a moment honoring her fallen comrade, and then it's time to move on.

What emotions will your character wrestle with in response to your All Is Lost?

Where and how can you show your protagonist debate?

The Dark Night Epiphany

This process of debate is also a time for discovery and learning. Maybe they get a peek into a pensieve (*Harry Potter*), are visited by a ghost, or just put the clues together. This is the time for your character's soul searching to uncover the missing piece they need to succeed.

What discovery or clue can your protagonist learn in their soul searching?

Return to familiar.

Remember when I talked about always moving forward? Well, now it's time for the exception that proves the rule. In this <u>beat</u>, it is totally fine, and maybe even expected, for the protagonist to move backward. After experiencing rejection, pain, fear, and suffering in the All is Lost, your protagonist may seek comfort in something familiar. Maybe they go back home, back to school, or return to their old job. It could be a less dramatic regression. Maybe they reach for an old mug, journal, or book that reminds them of their Act 1 world.

Unfortunately, this return to their past comforts is the opposite of comforting. She is back home with her parents, but time in Act 2 has made her independent and unwilling to bend to her mother's silly rules. He went back to the old job, but he is empty and unfulfilled now that he has been on this amazing adventure. That childhood mug she made with her father years ago shatters in her now superpowered grip. However you do it, use this "return to familiar" to highlight how much they have changed.

How does your protagonist "return to familiar" and why isn't it comforting?

How does your protagonist react? How does this highlight the change in your protagonist?

That is all there is to a great Dark Night of the Soul. Today they brood and tomorrow your character will break out of their funk and make the jump into Act 3! Set the moody music and get to writing!

John's Story John 14

What stands out most to you from John 14?

For days 23 to 26, we will dissect Jesus' last words before the cross instead of studying the way the passage fits into plot structure. If you care to understand why, check out this footnote.[a]

One last I AM. John 14:1-14

What three things does Jesus call himself in the I AM statement in verse 6?

Jesus tries to comfort His disciples, explaining He will return for them, but they are even more afraid. What does He mean when He says Peter will betray Him? Peter is the most zealous of the bunch. Thomas asks again; Peter must have been unclear. "Where are you going?"

It frustrates Jesus they still don't understand; by looking at Him, they are looking at the Father! *The Word on the Street*, which we affectionately call "the Gangster Bible," translates John 14:5-6 like this:

> Tom says, "Boss, if we knew where you're going, we might be able to work out the route, but we don't!"
> Jesus comes back with, "I'm the route, the true route. And I'm the energy to propel you along the route. I'm the only way you get to meet my dad."

---

[a] We are now in the throes of the hardest part of aligning plot structure with the Gospel of John. John 14 through 17 consist almost entirely of Jesus's last words, with occasional interruptions from His disciples. Even though these chapters contain foundational theology, John deviates from plot structure and disrupts pacing to include them.

To fully commit to keeping plot beats in the right place, all four chapters would fall in the Dark Night of the Soul. Then His arrest would be the Break into Three and the crucifixion/resurrection would stretch to fill the Five Point Finale. Implementing this pace in the Bible study would require an unmanageable amount of reading in one day and very little reading for the rest of the study.

Instead, I used His arrest for the High Tower Surprise. This means the Bible studies for Days 23 to 26 won't align with the plot structure discussions. This further proves the point I keep reiterating: **plot structures provide guidelines, not rules**. John knows how important this information is for his readers and sacrifices pacing to share it.

What does it mean that Jesus is "the way?" How does this impact your life?

What does it mean that Jesus is "the truth?" How does this impact your life?

What does it mean that Jesus is "the life?" How does this impact your life?

Help is on the way.   John 14:15-31

What help does Jesus promise will come?

How does Jesus say people who love Him will prove it? How does this look in your life?

How's your relationship with the Holy Spirit? How can you be more sensitive to His guidance?

The disciples didn't understand what it meant to receive the Holy Spirit, but we now know that this is God dwelling in us. Jesus did not leave us to walk alone, nor are we without guidance. But if we ignore the Holy Spirit, His voice can become hard for us to hear. Only by consistently trusting and listening can we grow in our ability to understand what He is saying in our hearts.

Remember, the Holy Spirit will never contradict the Word of God. If you hear something that contradicts scripture, it is not from the Holy Spirit. Bible study and prayer can help us grow in our sensitivity to His voice.

God's Story in Your Life

Who or what can you turn to as a voice of reason when you are struggling with a decision?

In what ways has your old familiar become unfamiliar?

What does this say about who you are becoming?

Daily Tracking Sheet ___ / ___ / ___

Today's writing goal is _____, which I will celebrate by _____.

I will connect with _____, by _____.

I will move my body by _____.

Today's Personal Goals:

1:

2:

3:

Reflection Questions

Today's Biggest Victory:

Today's Biggest Challenge and How I Overcame:

I am grateful for:

1:
2:
3:

Day 24: Break into 3

I am the vine; you are the branches. Whoever abides in me and I in him, he it is that bears much fruit, for apart from me you can do nothing. John 15:5

Writing Your Story

Your protagonist suffered through the All is Lost. They took a long, hard look at themselves in the Dark Night of the Soul. Now they are ready to recognize and address their internal flaw. This beat will feel very familiar to what we did back on Day 6 to break into Act 2. The difference is they broke into Act 2 without facing their fear or learning their lesson. Now, as we break into the third act, they have a similar single-scene beat where they prove their willingness to face their fear and fix things the right way.[a]

Your protagonist takes this action.

Like the Break into 2, it's important your story is pushed into Act 3 by your protagonist's choices. Passive protagonists pushed along by the story are dull and boring, making it difficult to care when they succeed or fail. Make sure your Break Into 3 is a decision and action taken by your protagonist, not something that happens to them.

How does your protagonist's choice break the story into Act 3?

The right idea, if not exactly the right choice.

Your character's decision, that led to Act 2, was based on evading their fear and trying to achieve their goal without learning their life lesson. This time, our hero knows the problem lies within them; after all, that's what the Dark Night of the Soul was all about. They aren't trying to run from their fear anymore and are now making a plan that shows they are not the same.

Although your protagonist is making a better choice, they can't yet make the best choice. After all, if you read ahead to the Five Point Finale, you know that their first plan isn't going to work. This plan should be better, and it should show they have grown and changed. But it can't quite be right, or we wouldn't need the third act.

How does your protagonist show they are learning their lesson and facing their fear?

What is the flaw in your protagonist's plan?

---

[a] In the Hero's Journey, this is called "the Return," because the character returns to their Act 1 world, but they are not the same. This feels very limiting to me because not every story ends with the hero back where they began. It isn't important whether your hero is "breaking" back into the Act 1 world, into a whole new world, or staying in the Act 2 world. What matters is that they make a decisive step that proves you have a new and improved protagonist, ready to face their fear and address their internal flaw.

John's Story   Read John 15

What stands out most to you from John 15?

Vine and Branches   John 15:1-17

Why is this important enough for Jesus to include in His last words?

What is the practical application of the vine and branches analogy?

Are you bearing fruit? How can you bear more fruit?

Hate from the World   John 15:18-27

Why is this important enough for Jesus to include in His last words?

How is this passage encouraging to the disciples? How does it encourage you?

What is the Holy Spirit's role? What is our role?

God's Story in Your Life

    Back on Day 6 we talked about practical steps you could take to "break" into your purpose. Think about what you have learned since Day 6 and what has changed.

What practical step can you take right now to recommit to your purpose?

Daily Tracking Sheet

___ / ___ / ___

Today's writing goal is _____, which I will celebrate by _____.

I will connect with _____, by _____.

I will move my body by _____.

Today's Personal Goals:

1:

2:

3:

Reflection Questions

Today's Biggest Victory:

Today's Biggest Challenge and How I Overcame:

I am grateful for:
1:
2:
3:

Day 25: Finale–Gathering the Team

Nevertheless, I tell you the truth: it is to your advantage that I go away, for if I do not go away, the Helper will not come to you. But if I go, I will send him to you. John 16:7

Writing Your Story

Well, here we are, we have broken through the barrier and arrived at the Finale. Hopefully, you have an idea what your Finale will be like, but we will spend the next five days discussing it. Since the Finale is where you tie it all together, don't try to rush. Without a solid Finale, reviews will say you didn't stick the landing on a great premise.

The Five Point Finale

Blake Snyder's Five Point Finale will provide us a framework for the next several days. While this is one great way to structure a finale, it is not the only way. Like everything in plot structure, these five "points" are guidelines and guardrails to help you map out and write your story. While you don't need a Five Point Finale, it is important to have elements from this, or other structures, so that your Finale doesn't fall flat.

As an introduction to the Five Point Finale, let's look at *Harry Potter and the Deathly Hallows*:

- **Break Into 3**: They break into Hogwarts to find the last horcrux.
- **Gathering The Team**: The team gathers in the Room of Requirement. They share the plan with the rest of Dumbledore's Army and then delegate tasks to individuals.
- **Executing The Plan**: The battle starts. Ron and Hermione destroy the cup with a basilisk fang. Harry finds, and destroys, the diadem. Voldemort's army is, at least temporarily, pushed back.
- **The High Tower Surprise**: Snape dies and gives Harry his memories. Voldemort announces he will wait one hour. If Harry doesn't come into the forest alone, everyone will be killed.
- **Dig Deep Down**: Harry watches Snape's memories and learns what he must do to defeat Voldemort. He goes into the forest, where dead people he loves give him the courage to sacrifice himself.
- **The Execution of the New Plan**: Harry meets Voldemort and sacrifices himself. He goes to King's Cross and speaks with Dumbledore. He sees the shriveled soul of Voldemort. He returns to his body, the true master of death. Nevel kills the snake, Molly kills Bellatrix, and Harry's battle with Voldemort finally ends with the Dark Lord dead. Harry returns the Elder Wand to Dumbledore's tomb.

Don't worry if that seems like a lot. We have five days to break that down and make sense of it. Today we are going to look at Gathering the Team. Your hero is ready to do it. They made it out of the Dark Night of the Soul and broke themselves into Act 3. No more thinking about it. Time to go. But first, we must prepare.

Gathering and preparation

Your hero needs to gather what needs gathering. This will probably include assembling a team of people. But it could also involve gathering supplies, developing plans, and various other details.

- Who needs to be on the team?
- What plans do they need to make?
- What do they need to make, prepare, or pack?
- What skills do they need to learn or practice?

What and who needs to be "gathered" or prepared before executing the plan?

Restoring relationships.

Any bridges burned back in the All is Lost beat need to be rebuilt. Your protagonist already mended the relationship he had with himself in the Dark Night of The Soul, but now it's time to go back and make amends with others. If this is a relationship story (like a love story), it's not yet time to heal the key romantic relationship; that will come later. But they may have, for example, injured a friendship that needs mending.

What relationships need to be restored before executing the plan?

John's Story   Read John 16

What stands out most to you from John 16?

The Holy Spirit's job.   John 16:1-15

Why is this important enough for Jesus to include in His last words?

Why does Jesus say it is for their good He goes away? Do the disciples agree? Do you agree?

What can we learn about difficulty from these words?

Grief will become Joy   John 16:16-24

Why is this important enough for Jesus to include in His last words?

How did Jesus explaining this in advance give His disciples peace after His death?

Getting literal
John 16:25-33

Why does Jesus say that a time is coming He will no longer speak figuratively?

Why is Jesus exasperated by the disciples' response?

How does knowing Jesus has overcome the world give you peace?

God's Story in Your Life

Yesterday we talked about a step you could take into deeper commitment toward your purpose. With commitment comes the need for tools, skills, and even people. Maybe you need supplies to cook a meal for your ministry team or you need to learn Spanish to better reach the underserved in your community. Maybe there are people you need on your team that have skills you don't. For example, I need to find an illustrator!

What tools, lessons, or people do you need to "gather" to maintain progress on your purpose?

I am often guilty of pinging someone on Microsoft Teams and starting with what I need instead of a greeting. You probably don't have the same personality flaw. But no matter the person, everyone's personality can eventually irritate others. If not addressed, small misunderstandings can escalate into significant relationship issues. Working together frequently or under pressure can make this worse.

In pursuing your purpose, what relationships have "worn thin" from conflicts or disagreements?

Where do you need to apologize? Who do you need to forgive?

One way to insulate relationships from minor offenses is to plan "downtime" together. Set aside time to enjoy each other, instead of every interaction being about delivering results or striving toward a goal. If you haven't recently, schedule an event for your team to enjoy each other's company.

Another way to guard against minor offenses derailing teams is to refocus on the purpose. Be intentional to connect the details of everyone's work to the larger, shared goal. This helps remind everyone what really matters.

What proactive measures can you take to protect your key relationships?

Daily Tracking Sheet ___ / ___ / ___

Today's writing goal is _____, which I will celebrate by _____.

I will connect with _____, by _____.

I will move my body by _____.

Today's Personal Goals:

1:

2:

3:

Reflection Questions

Today's Biggest Victory:

Today's Biggest Challenge and How I Overcame:

I am grateful for:

1:

2:

3:

Week 5 Discussion and Review

Therefore, since we are surrounded by so great a cloud of witnesses, let us also lay aside every weight, and sin which clings so closely, and let us run with endurance the race that is set before us, Hebrews 12:1

Story Check-In

How is writing going?

What has gone well? What one sentence are you most proud of or want to share?

Where did you get stuck or where do you need feedback?

Bible Study Check-In

What most surprised you from John 13-16?

Who do you relate most with in the foot washing scene?
  (Jesus, Peter, Judas, or the other disciples)

How can you serve people well, even when they are not kind to you?

How do you hope people respond when you serve them? How do you respond when others serve you?

God's Story in Your Life

Describe an "All is Lost" moment in your past and how you overcame it.

What hurt or habit is holding you back right now from taking the next step in your purpose?

Pray and Close

Pray for endurance to finish the work you started as you go into the last week of this study.

Pray for the relationships you have with each other and with the people you serve alongside.

My notes and doodles:

Day 26: Finale–Executing the Plan

"I do not ask for these only, but also for those who will believe in me through their word, that they may all be one, just as you, Father, are in me, and I in you," John 17:20-21a

Writing Your Story

This is the last week! Can you believe it? You are almost there. Hopefully, the excitement and momentum will help propel you through these last several days. No matter what happens, keep going. Let any cleanup wait for your second draft.

Your protagonist and their team are as prepared as they are going to be. We have the plan, and it's probably crazy, but they will make it work. Executing the Plan is the fun part of the Climax. It's where everything goes (mostly) right.

Payoff the Setups

It's time to fire any Chekhov's guns still lying around that haven't yet discharged. Remember that obscure skill with speaking the made-up language? Time to pay that off by having the team use it to communicate without tipping off the enemy. Was there a special weapon, facial expression, codeword, tool, handshake, or anything else that you have set up? How can that pay off as they execute the plan?

What have you set up in your story that still needs to be paid off?

Let the team shine.

Although this is the Finale, it is not yet the big hero moment for your protagonist (that will come later). Now is the time to let the side characters each have their moment to shine. Show the reader why those characters are so vital to the hero's success and give them their opportunity for the spotlight.

In the Climax of *Heartless*, all three of Catherine's friends play a part. Raven goes to rescue Mary Ann. Hatta gets Jest's hat, which Catherine pulls the sword from so that Jest can kill the Jabberwock. This shows the reader why all four of them had to walk through the door; Catherine couldn't have rescued Mary Ann alone.

Who needs their moment to shine?

How can they do that as a part of executing the plan?

Sacrifice or step aside.

We need to isolate the hero so they can have their big moment. During a wedding ceremony, the father of a bride says, "Her mother and I" (his moment to shine), then steps aside so the groom (the hero) can take his place. Your side characters will do their part (shine) and then step aside to let the hero take center stage.

Sometimes they do their part and are already "aside," like a programmer who hacks the cameras but spends the rest of the Finale in the van. Other side characters may be pushed aside, injured, or even dead. Some will make a sacrifice (as their moment to shine) that puts them out of commission (step aside). To give the hero space for their big ending, we need to move the side characters out of the way.

How can your team "step aside" to make room for the hero to shine?

Who could/should make a sacrifice? How would that play out?

John's Story   Read John 17
What stands out most to you from John 17?

John 17 is often called the "High Priestly Prayer" and is the longest recorded prayer Jesus prays in the Bible. Where the Lord's Prayer provides an example to us of how to structure a prayer, this chapter gives us insight into what topics Jesus prayed about.

Jesus prays for God's glory.   John 17:1-5
How often do you pray for God to be glorified by an action you are about to take?

If you prayed this more often, how would it change your decisions?

Jesus prays for our safety.   John 17:6-19
Does this prayer apply to us or only the disciples?

Why doesn't Jesus want God to rescue us from the world?

Jesus prays for us to walk in unity   John 17:20-26
How does His prayer for unity relate to His prayer we share God with the world?

What can you do today to walk in unity or share God's love with the world?

God's Story in Your Life

What "set up" in your life have you not pulled the trigger on?

How can you reject <u>fear</u>, and Execute the Plan?

Who needs their moment to shine?

How can you encourage them to use their unique gifts?

What kind of sacrifice(s) will your purpose require?

Are you willing to make that sacrifice?

Daily Tracking Sheet ___ / ___ / ___

Today's writing goal is _____, which I will celebrate by _____.

I will connect with _____, by _____.

I will move my body by _____.

Today's Personal Goals:

1:

2:

3:

Reflection Questions

Today's Biggest Victory:

Today's Biggest Challenge and How I Overcame:

I am grateful for:

1:

2:

3:

Day 27: Finale—The High Tower Surprise

Peter again denied it, and at once a rooster crowed. John 18:27

Writing Your Story

Here we are, in the last moments of the story. Everything is going well for the hero. The team has all had their moment to shine, and it looks like they are about to win. In fact, why did it seem that this plan was impossible? Everything is going great. Then… what? Well, we can't just win like that! We want our characters to earn this victory, so we need to throw one last brutal failure in their lap.

Peter beheads Jest (*Heartless*). The Nazgul give Aragon Frodo's mithril shirt and Sam's sword, proving (as far as they know) that there is no hope (*Return of the King*). The bomb goes off and everyone dies (*Ready Player One*). But it doesn't have to be an action story to deliver a gut punch to your protagonist in the finale. Bob Ewell attacks Scout and Jim (*To Kill a Mockingbird*). Bailey dies (*The Sisterhood of the Traveling Pants*).

Punch them in the gut.

The protagonist doesn't need a physical punch, but this twist should hit hard. It should make the plan, which was working against all odds, totally unravel. Whatever the twist, this needs to hurt. The protagonist has gone all in, done everything they think they should, and it isn't enough. They have failed.

How can you "sucker punch" your protagonist by hitting them where it hurts the most?

Isolate the hero.

The hero needs to go the last bit alone. In *Ready Player One*, when the sixers detonated the bomb that killed everyone, Wade survives because of the extra life he won playing Pac Man. Now he can go through the third gate, but he is all alone. Then he is isolated further because communication with his team is severed. This final test, he will have to win on his own.

How can you isolate your hero?

We don't just want the hero to be alone; we want the hero to **feel** alone. Think about when Elijah claims he is the only person still faithful to the Lord (1 Kings 19:10). Just one chapter ago, he learned of 100 others (1 Kings 18:22), but he feels alone in his fight against Jezebel.

What can you do to make your protagonist feel more alone than they really are?

The traitor

One way to sucker punch and isolate your protagonist is to have someone betray them. Today we will talk about some ways to execute a betrayal well. These same scenarios can also work, with a little tweaking, in the All is Lost.

Traitor Type	Example	Setting It Up
The guy who was always going to be a traitor.	Greg joined the party at the very beginning, but he never wanted to take down the Dark Lord. He knew this prophesied hero would find the Dark Lord. Greg seeks to earn a seat beside the new master of the universe by betraying the hero to him.	If this is the betrayal you have been planning all along, then there should be hints that Greg was never fully part of the team. This is not a choice you can believably make this late into the story without major rewrites.
The broken bridge that wasn't really mended.	Henry came back when the hero apologized, but he was only pretending everything was alright. While away, he learned he could get revenge (and a payday) by playing along and delivering the unsuspecting hero to the enemy.	Something should be a bit "off" during the Gathering the Team. They also would not be doing their part during Executing the Plan.
The one who couldn't, or wouldn't, pay the price of loyalty.	Sarah believes in the mission and even dreams of marrying our hero. But the Dark Lord has her father and is threatening to kill him if she doesn't do as she's told. She cannot pay that price, even if it means her beloved hero will fail. Travis is glad to be part of this mission. But when he's offered a million dollars to rat out the team, he takes the guaranteed money, and his skin, over loyalty.	Point to this trait that they value throughout the story. Sarah should display willingness to sacrifice anything for her family. Travis should show other acts of cowardice or greed.
The accidental traitor.	Jackie's obsession with posting on Instagram has given the enemy an easy way to track the team's movements. Travis messages with a girl on Tinder, unaware "she" is really the mafia boss. Shelia has location sharing turned on with her Google account and doesn't even realize it's giving them away.	The audience should know about the character trait or quirk that results in the betrayal. Jackie is always on Instagram, Travis goes on and on about this girl, and Shelia is clueless around technology.
	This will be more powerful if you make the hero believe it was not an accident. Remember, this is about kicking your hero, hard, one last time. Making this feel personal is easier if the betrayal appears, at least to the protagonist, to be intentional.	

What kind of betrayal works in your story?

Quick Note: If you are thinking, "I need to go rewrite this character…" don't let that derail you! Make notes for your second draft and keep going. You are almost at the end. Finish and fix it during editing. Changing an unfinished story can keep you from ever finishing.

John's Story   John 18

What stands out most to you from John 18?

What kind of traitor is Judas? How was this foreshadowed earlier in John?

How does Jesus respond to Judas' betrayal?

What kind of traitor is Peter? How was this foreshadowed earlier in John?

How does Jesus respond to Peter's betrayal?

Betrayal is hard. The closer you are to a person, the harder their turning away is to handle. Judas was always going to betray Jesus; he was not happy about Jesus' disinterest in overthrowing Rome.[a] But Peter was one of Jesus' three guys. He was in the inner circle. John makes a point of telling us that Jesus looked at Peter. He does not look away. That is powerful! Even when we fail Him, He never turns away from us.

God's Story in Your Life

Just like we discussed in the writing portion, there are many types and ways that those we love can betray us. Sometimes betrayal is malicious. More often, people leave because of the natural ebb and flow of life. God takes them in a new direction, and you're left holding the project, group, or team without their support.

Have you ever been betrayed? By whom? What kind of betrayal was it? How did you respond?

How should you respond based on Jesus' example?

After suffering through a betrayal, it's hard to love again. Whether someone leaves because they develop other interests, move, die, or are truly malicious, the pain of seeing them walk away can harden our hearts against future relationships. But God did not create us to do life alone. Don't let past hurts keep you from living in biblical community.

How can you press into relationships after suffering loss or betrayal?

Are you in community now?

---

[a] Some believe Judas thought Jesus' arrest would "force His hand" to overthrow Rome. Even if this is true, it's still a betrayal.

Daily Tracking Sheet   __ / __ / __

Today's writing goal is _____, which I will celebrate by _____.

I will connect with _____, by _____.

I will move my body by _____.

Today's Personal Goals:

1:

2:

3:

Reflection Questions

Today's Biggest Victory:

Today's Biggest Challenge and How I Overcame:

I am grateful for:

1:
2:
3:

Day 28: Finale–Dig Deep Down

Pilate also wrote an inscription and put it on the cross. It read, "Jesus of Nazareth, the King of the Jews."
John 19:19

Writing Your Story

Your hero has taken one too many hits. The plan has failed. His team is gone. It's game over. But this time, the hero isn't willing to give up. He's hurt, physically and emotionally, but he's no longer the coward we met in the Opening Image, and he won't be running away from this fight. Instead, he is ready to Dig Deep Down and find something inside himself that he didn't know was there.

A voice of hope.

Although your hero is alone, it doesn't mean they are without help. Sometimes a spiritual figure, such as an angel, helps them. Elijah hears the voice of God on a mountain and realizes he isn't the last prophet of God in Israel. Harry communes with the ghosts of those he loves in the forest to find the courage to sacrifice himself to destroy Voldemort's last horcrux.[a]

What kind of spiritual encounter would help your hero make the right (or wrong) choice?

Finding the strength... or not.

Like the Debate in Act 1 and the Dark Night of the Soul, we slow down to give the B Story, inside your hero, time to shine through. But this is in the middle of the story's Finale, so don't pause for too long. They already debated and found strength in the Dark Night of the Soul. Yes, this was a harder blow than before, but they are stronger. It's time for them to decide to get up and prove they learned their lesson.

Or maybe they don't. Maybe they dig down and decide that there isn't anything inside, and they have nothing left to give. The High Tower Surprise pushed too hard. They have fallen too far, and redemption is no longer possible.

What decision does your hero make?

It's about theme!

The A Story and B Story have grown more and more connected throughout the second half. But this decision is 100% B Story. It's not about their training, weapons, plans, magical abilities, or anything else related to the A Story. Overcoming this last hurdle requires them to learn their life lesson, overcome their fatal flaw, reject their misbelief, and face their fear. These all mean the same thing: they must prove they learned your story's theme.

How does your hero's choice prove they have (or haven't) learned the theme?

---

[a] Not every story has this type of help. If you choose to include it, make sure it conforms to the established rules of your story.

John's Story John 19

What stands out most to you from John 19?

Jesus is dead. "But wait," you say, "I thought this was a retrospective beat where we dig deep down so we can make the right move in the next scene?" Yes, you are right; gold star for you. Remember, Jesus isn't the one who needs to learn a lesson. John makes a point of this in the way he covers the crucifixion. Very little emphasis of these scenes is on Jesus. Instead, John focuses on character moments for those around Him.

Pilate John 19:1-22

Ultimately, we don't know if Pilate believed in Jesus or was doing this to spite the Jewish leaders because they forced him into a difficult situation. It is possible to read this and believe that Pilate believed in, or at least respected, Jesus.[24] What is clear is Pilate gave Jesus over to be crucified because of his fear of the crowd, not because he believed Jesus deserved death.

How does fear of other's opinions keep you from walking in faith?

The Jewish leaders John 19:1-22

The Jewish leaders know Jesus shows signs from God. They, more than anyone, should see that prophesies are being fulfilled in their midst. Perhaps they knew Jesus was the Messiah but hardened their heart because He threatened their power and wealth.[a] Maybe they were so blinded with fervor for the religious traditions that they couldn't see God right in front of them. Either way, they chose their power, rituals, wealth, and status over faith.

What things (tangible or intangible) keep you from walking in faith?

The soldiers John 19:23-24, 31-37

All three Synoptic Gospels include a centurion who professes faith that Jesus was the Son of God.[b] But John focuses on soldiers who are too distracted fighting over Jesus' clothes to see God in front of them.

How does striving after things keep you from seeing what God is doing in front of you?

---

[a] On Day 4 we talked about how they were making a lot of money in their position, mostly by taking advantage of the poor and foreigners.
[b] Matthew 27:54, Mark 15:39, and Luke 23:47.

John and Mary　　　　　　　　　　　　　　　　　　　　　　　John 19:25-27

I have always found this passage confusing. After all, Jesus isn't Mary's only son.[a] Why does Jesus "give" Mary to John from the cross? The commentaries I read had various explanations,[b] but all agree that, regardless of Jesus' reasons, John and Mary obeyed.

This is a moment of confusion and pain, when everything is going differently than they wanted and expected. But Jesus speaks a command into that chaos, and they obey immediately.[c] They don't argue; Mary doesn't explain she has other sons who can take care of her. They just obey.

What has God asked you to do that you can act on today?

Joseph of Arimathea　　　　　　　　　　　　　　　　　　　John 19:38-42

Joseph and Pilate have a fear of people in common. In fact, they fear the same people (the religious leaders). But Joseph acts, despite his fear, and because of his faith we have an empty tomb.[d]

How can you act in faith despite the fear you listed on the prior page?

God's Story in Your Life

By now, you have probably figured out the cadence to this whole story thing. There is a trigger (Catalyst, All is Lost, High Tower Surprise). Then there is contemplation (Debate, Dark Night of the Soul, Dig Deep Down). After that, the protagonist acts (Break Into 2, Break Into 3, Execution of the New Plan). Even in a smaller sense, the cadence of a single scene has this trigger–debate–action formula.

Your story of pursuing your purpose will be no different. You will move forward, encounter an obstacle, wrestle with the repercussions, and then choose to act in faith to keep going (or give up on faith and quit). Every success story is riddled with setbacks and obstacles the hero overcomes. So is every failure story. Life is hard.

Go read the story of someone who has experienced success. It can be a ministry founder, entrepreneur, or athlete. Draw inspiration as you read about the obstacles they overcame and save it for the next time you need a "Voice of Hope."

Who did you read about?[e] What obstacles did they overcome on the way to success?

How has reading their story helped you have faith and confidence to keep moving forward?

---

[a] The book of James was written by one of Jesus' brothers. See also Mark 3:31-32, Matthew 12:46-47, or Luke 8:19-20.
[b] Some explanations given: To emphasize the reordered relationships in the kingdom of God. To honor John, the only disciple present. His siblings were not yet believers. He knew John, as the only disciple who died a natural death, would outlast His siblings. John was His closest friend. Jesus knew John would stay in Jerusalem during the diaspora caused by the church's persecution.
[c] I say "immediately" because many translations say, "from that hour," indicating the obedience was not delayed.
[d] Without Joseph, they would have thrown Jesus' body in a common grave. This would mean no empty tomb after the resurrection.
[e] For ideas, check out the A21 or Colin's Hope story. I linked to both stories on Day 4, when we discussed the Catalyst.

Daily Tracking Sheet   __ / __ / __

Today's writing goal is _____, which I will celebrate by _____.

I will connect with _____, by _____.

I will move my body by _____.

Today's Personal Goals:

1:

2:

3:

Reflection Questions

Today's Biggest Victory:

Today's Biggest Challenge and How I Overcame:

I am grateful for:
1:
2:
3:

Day 29: Finale–Execution of the New Plan

Jesus said to him, "Have you believed because you have seen me? Blessed are those who have not seen and yet have believed." John 20:29

Writing Your Story

Here we are! We have reached the best part. Despite being beaten, crushed, and battered on all sides, our hero persisted and kept getting back up. Now it's time for him to have the success he has worked so hard to earn.[a] We have reached the last point in our Five Point Finale so let's finally slay that Dark Lord!

What makes a great story? Why are there some we enjoy and then toss aside and others we come back to again and again? How does one book end up forgotten by time and another book become a classic that is taught in the classroom? It can't be the sky beams, magic powers, or superhuman feats, or none of us would have read *To Kill a Mockingbird*. Neither can it be the lack of them, or we wouldn't consider *The Lord of the Rings* a classic.

I will never be a weightless elf in Lothlorien, a witch learning spells at Hogwarts, or a girl living in the antebellum south before the Civil War. Still, when I read *The Lord of the Rings*, *Harry Potter*, or *Gone with the Wind*, I resonate with these stories. They move me deep inside.

While I have never lived in a magic forest, I know how it feels to long for a beauty that is slowly being eaten by modernization. I have never waved a wand, yet I resonate with the theme of sacrificial love and hope I would be as brave as Harry. Although I have never faced the challenges that Scarlet survived, I have experienced striving so hard to succeed that I forgot to be happy.

Now is the time to pay off all the buildup in your story. You have taken your character on a physical journey, but also on an internal quest. They decided yesterday and today they act on it. But this time they find success. The ring is destroyed. Voldemort dies. Or maybe they don't. Rhett leaves Scarlett, just as she finally realizes that she loves him. Whether your hero succeeds or fails, what matters most is how this success or failure plays out the life lesson and theme you have woven throughout your story.

How does your story end? How does this success or failure prove your book's theme?

Unlike other plot structures, the BS2 includes the wrap up in the last point of the Five Point Finale, instead of separating the Climax and the Falling Action. The BS2 would consider all scenes in *The Lord of the Rings* from the destruction of the ring until we see Frodo board the ship to Valinor as a part of the Finale. I think I know why Blake did this: it reminds us that each scene should resonate with the theme.

What scenes do you need to wrap up loose ends?

How does each scene they tie back to your theme?

---

[a] Or maybe he fails. We will get to that soon enough.

John's Story — John 20:1-29

What stands out most to you from John 20:1-29?

This is what we all came for: He is risen! But why is the resurrection so important? Death is not natural; God did not create us to die. Death is the payment due for sin. Because Jesus never sinned, death had no authority over Him. Thus, He had the power to defeat death and, in doing so, He gives us the ability to find life in Him!

But John's theme isn't about Jesus rising from the dead, it's about belief. In this chapter, where Jesus raises from the dead, He doesn't own the spotlight. Instead, like with the crucifixion, John focuses on how several people respond to the resurrected Jesus.

John believes. — John 20:3-10

What does John 20:8 tell us about John's theme for his Gospel?

Peter and John have this footrace, which is one of my favorite anecdotes in the Bible.[a] But the point isn't who wins the footrace. The point is what we see at the end of verse 8. John does not see the resurrected Jesus, just an empty tomb, and he believes. Sometimes faith is as simple as that; you see evidence of God in the world around you and believe.

Mary Magdalene believes. — John 20:11-18

Jesus' resurrection is the most important event in the entire story. Without this, our faith means nothing. Thus, it would stand to reason that the first person to see Him would be an important person, or at least a disciple. But God continues to turn our worldly expectations on their head.

The disciples left (v10) but Mary Magdalene stayed behind. She is distraught. Once demon possessed, Jesus freed her (Luke 8) and changed her life's trajectory. She's devastated by His death and now further shattered because she cannot honor His body.

How does Jesus reveal himself to Mary Magdalene?

Mary Magdalene is too caught up in her grief to notice Jesus, believing Him to be a gardener. Jesus doesn't reveal himself with a miracle, a sermon, or a rebuke for her lack of faith. It isn't the sound of His voice or sight of His face that alerts her she is speaking to Jesus.[b] She doesn't recognize Him until He says her name. Mary Magdalene believes in a moment of personal intimacy.

---

[a] John makes a point of explaining that he reached the tomb first, even though Peter went into the tomb before him. This seemingly silly anecdote feels like He is setting straight a debate among friends. It makes me laugh at the humanity of Peter and John. They were ordinary people, just like us!

[b] In verse 13, Jesus speaks to Mary, but she still doesn't recognize Him. She sees Him without recognizing Him. It is possible that He looked different, as He is now in a new, resurrected body. Alternatively, Mary could have been too overwhelmed with sorrow to notice her miracle standing right there.

The disciples believe. John 20:19-25a

What are Jesus' first words to His disciples? Why is this necessary?

The religious leaders killed their rabi and someone stole the body.[a] They huddle behind a locked door and wonder what should be done. Jesus appears and shows himself to the disciples in the room where they are hiding.[b] He shows the wounds in His hands and side. The disciples believe after seeing the resurrected Jesus.

Thomas believes. John 20:24-29

Thomas gets a bad rap. Heck, we even call him "doubting Thomas" because he didn't believe the crazy story that was told by the disciples. But remember, those same disciples didn't believe until after they saw the proof Thomas asked for. It's not his fault the daily grocery run fell to him right as Jesus was getting ready to show up.

Why does John include this story about Thomas? What does it illustrate or illuminate for us?

Do you believe? John 20:29

John's entire premise is that we must believe to find life in Jesus. It is not enough that He died and rose from the dead for our sins. We must accept salvation by believing in Jesus as the lamb of God. Jesus is speaking about us when He says, "blessed are those who have not seen and yet have believed."[c]

Do you believe in Jesus as your personal savior? Why or why not?

You might be like John and believe once you see evidence of God in the world around you. Maybe you are like Mary, finding belief in a moment of intimacy. Maybe, like the disciples, you need a personal miracle. If you are like Thomas, and not sure about this whole Jesus thing, know that He will meet you where you are. Kudos to you for staying with this study; don't stop when it ends. Keep seeking. You will find!

Despite trusting Jesus as my savior, I still go through seasons of struggling to believe God. I strive to be good enough on my own. But salvation is through grace by faith, not through work by perfection. God did not come to make bad people good, but to make dead people alive. Cease striving to qualify and rest in the confidence that you are already enough.

---

[a] Sure, some woman claims to have seen Him, but she is just a woman; her words wouldn't even stand in court.
[b] Again, the door is locked. They do not feel safe.
[c] John 20:29b NIV

Do you really believe Jesus is enough?

God's Story in Your Life

I don't know where you are today in your quest to live out the purpose God laid out for your life. Maybe you are in the final chapters of a big dream and maybe you are on the third restart after yet another devastating setback. Perhaps everything you thought you wanted isn't working out and God is opening a new door down a different path. Or maybe you are just in the grind, somewhere lost in the middle of Act 2 and wondering if you will ever make it.

Don't give up. I am thrilled to be where I am, but it's not what I expected. My passion to wake people up to the purpose God engraved in their hearts has never wavered. But it wasn't until after I gave up on my old plan that God gave me the idea to write this study. As long as I fought to hold on to my goal, my purpose stayed stagnant. When I let go of my plan, God showed me His.

What has changed in the "plan" since you started pursuing your purpose?

Where are you clinging to your own plan instead of holding on to your purpose?

Daily Tracking Sheet   __ / __ / __

Today's writing goal is _____, which I will celebrate by _____.

I will connect with _____, by _____.

I will move my body by _____.

Today's Personal Goals:

1:

2:

3:

Reflection Questions

Today's Biggest Victory:

Today's Biggest Challenge and How I Overcame:

I am grateful for:
1:
2:
3:

Day 30: Final Image

Now Jesus did many other signs in the presence of the disciples, which are not written in this book; but these are written so that you may believe that Jesus is the Christ, the Son of God, and that by believing you may have life in his name. John 20:30-31

Writing Your Story

Well, here we are, on day 30 of this wild ride. It's not quite time to pop the champagne and launch the firecrackers. Don't hang up your sneakers at the 26-mile marker and miss the last .2 miles to earn your medal. We still have one more scene to write today and, although it isn't long, it is vital to satisfying your readers with a clear ending to the story. We are, of course, talking about the Final Image.

Like a mirror to the Opening Image, this is the last scene you leave your readers with before fading to black. This image has a lot riding on it, so let's look at what you need.

Close your story with a reminder of your theme.

Remember your theme, that important life truth that made you want to write this story? Well, make sure you fade out on an image that drives your message home. Did you want people to believe in the power of friendship? Then there should be friendship in this last scene. Was the point of the story that anyone can be a hero by doing small acts of kindness? End with someone doing something heroic, like putting away someone else's trash or grocery cart.

Whatever the message of your story, tuck that lesson back into your Final Image. Don't have a preacher come out to give a heavy-handed sermon. Instead, use this scene as a gentle reminder. "Hey, remember we had a point here? Yeah, that was intentional."

How can you include your theme in your Final Image?

Prove your protagonist has learned their life lesson.

You have taken your protagonist on a journey through a lot of pain and heartache, so you could shake them out of the stupor that kept them living with their fatal flaw. They have faced their fear, addressed their misbelief, and learned their lesson. They have succeeded and failed and succeeded and failed their way to a Finale that hinged on their decision to learn this oh-so-important lesson.

Now they have reached the end of their journey. Maybe they won, and now they are celebrating their victory. Maybe they lost, and the lesson they learned came from the ashes of defeat. Either way, they are not the same bright-eyed adventurer who embarked on this quest in the Opening Image.

Was she afraid of confrontation? Now she should stand up for herself. Was he unable to resist a bargain, even though he had financial struggles and enough junk to make traversing his home nearly impossible? Show him turning down the deal of a lifetime.

How can you show your protagonist has (or hasn't) learned their life lesson?

Close your story with a mirror of your Opening Image.

Their new world might be their old world and might not. Maybe they got everything they wanted, and maybe they didn't. Perhaps they learned their lesson, and perhaps not. Whatever the outcome, they are not the same. This journey has transformed your protagonist.

Many successful stories highlight this change by using a Final Image that mirrors the Opening Image. We see the same family dinner with the same awkward conversation from the same assortment of odd people. But this time the protagonist is no longer suffering in silence under their ridicule. Now, she is self-confident and engaged. Or maybe now she dominates the table, having taken the head seat since the dinner is now hosted at her home.

Another way to do this is to create a mirror of the scene in a whole new world. No longer does he sit at the head of an empty table counting his coins alone in a cold house. Now he sits at a bustling Christmas dinner shared with family and friends, having learned his lesson from the three ghosts of Christmas.

How can your Final Image mirror the scene from your Opening Image?

You made it! Great work! Write "The End" and let everyone know you finished. Whether it took you thirty days or three years, you made it to the end and that's something to be proud of! I am so thankful to have had the privilege of being a part of this journey with you.

John's Story   Read John 20:30-31

What stands out most to you from John 20:30-31?

No, that wasn't a mistake. Yes, we only have two verses today. But even in these two verses, John totally nails the Final Image. Let's ask those same three questions to see how.

How does John include his <u>theme</u> in this passage?

How does John show the disciples have overcome their unbelief?

How does John mirror the Opening Image with this Final Image?

This verse is all about belief, so that first question is easy! While the individual disciples aren't mentioned by name here, John makes a point of saying they saw many other signs, and shares these, so we will believe. This implies that the disciples had more than enough evidence to believe. As for the mirror, what I notice most is the way John takes a "zoomed out" approach to the story, much like those early verses in John.

I recognize there may be some confusion about why we did John 20 for the Final Image instead of John 21. This is because John 21 is an Epilogue, so I wrote a bonus lesson for tomorrow!

God's Story in Your Life

We have spent the last 30 days talking about the purpose God has for your life and the story He is telling through your purpose. Maybe you are celebrating the successful completion of your goal and maybe you are still early in Act 2.

Wherever you are in your story, there is value in taking time to reflect on how far you have come.

What has been the <u>theme</u> of your life since starting this study?

What lesson(s) have you learned?

How does your today look similar to when you started?

How does your life today look different?

Daily Tracking Sheet ___ / ___ / ___

Today's writing goal is _____, which I will celebrate by _____.

I will connect with _____, by _____.

I will move my body by _____.

Today's Personal Goals:

1:

2:

3:

Reflection Questions

Today's Biggest Victory:

Today's Biggest Challenge and How I Overcame:

I am grateful for:

1:
2:
3:

Bonus Day: Epilogue

Peter, and some disciples were chilling after these events. Peter announced, "I'm going fishing." Everyone thought that sounded like a great idea and decided to tag along. John 21:2-3[a]

Writing Your Story

You made it! What's that? You thought we were done? Well, we finished the plot, and you wrote your story. But John isn't over because John wrote an epilogue. Epilogues are not really part of the story; they are like the after-credits scene in a Marvel movie. If you skip them, you can still enjoy and understand the movie you watched. Staying through the credits is worth it because you get a glimpse of where the story is going next, a new character, or a joke's resolution.

To decide if an epilogue fits your story, ask yourself these questions:

Is there another book to tease?

Just because your book has a sequel doesn't mean you need an Epilogue. None of the *Harry Potter* books have epilogues. But if your story continues, an epilogue may be helpful. You can use it to introduce that next villain or refocus attention on a side character who will be the protagonist in the next book.

Are there unanswered questions you want to clarify?

By "unanswered questions," I mean information not vital to enjoying the story. Perhaps your book was excerpts from an old diary, and you want to show your audience how the diary was "found" or published.

Is there a funny or special moment that didn't fit in the story?

Maybe you just want that fancy wedding scene that didn't quite fit in the story. Maybe you have your own version of the shawarma scene in Avengers, to give your reader a chuckle on the way out by paying off a joke you set up in chapter 12. Or maybe there is a scene that was chef's-kiss-perfect but messed up the story's pacing. They say to kill your darlings, but maybe this one can become the epilogue.[b]

Is the scene you are imagining really your Final Image?

Harry Potter and the Deathly Hallows doesn't end in the aftermath of the Battle of Hogwarts. Instead, JK Rowling jumps 19 years into the future. She wants to end her story about the power of love on a positive note. But right after a brutal, bloody war isn't really the fuzzy socks and hot chocolate feeling she was going for. Despite the time jump, her last chapter is not an Epilogue; it is her Final Image. Without that scene, the story is incomplete.

If you are considering an Epilogue, weigh carefully if this scene instead belongs in your story. Think back to the three pieces of a Final Image we discussed yesterday and compare them to what you have in mind. If they fit, probably drop the Epilogue, and make this the last chapter.

What type of epilogue (if any) fits in your story?

---

[a] This is obviously not word for word from the Bible in any translation. I wrote it this way for comedic effect.
[b] Marissa Meyer often includes a scene that didn't fit the story's pacing as bonus material in the back of her books.

Epilogue | 131

John's Story

Read John 21

What stands out most to you from John 21?

While John doesn't introduce any new characters, this chapter has many characteristics of an epilogue. The rest of John is about Jesus and showing us who He is. But here, John shifts the focus to the disciples, especially Peter, one of the two "main" characters of the New Testament. John 21 comes after a perfect Final Image, shifts focus to Peter, and has the bros out fishing. Sounds like an epilogue! But why were they fishing? It was familiar. When we are uncomfortable, we reach out for the familiar.

Who instigated this fishing trip? Why was he uncomfortable?

Peter denied Jesus three times, and he's carrying around the weight of that mistake. Thomas, one chapter ago, doubted Jesus's resurrection. They were all afraid of the religious leaders, who murdered Jesus. So, they pack the cooler, haul out the old fishing boat, and have a guy's day on the water.

What do you run to for comfort when you are stressed, tired, overwhelmed, or feeling guilty?

God does not begrudge us our days off. Jesus doesn't show up and give them a lesson on discipline and responsibility. He doesn't scold them for returning to the fishing boats they left behind to follow Him. We don't serve a striving God and we aren't called to be constantly busy, burned out, and burdened. But when we take needs only Jesus can fill to these broken cisterns,[a] we will never find satisfaction.

They fished all night and caught no fish. Jesus supplies a miraculous catch of fish. He was reminding Peter of his salvation experience (Luke 5:2-11). Jesus made a fire. But not just any fire; it is an *anthrakia* (charcoal) fire. We only find this Greek word twice in the Gospels, both in John. The other is in John 18:18.

After they eat, Jesus gets to the real reason He has crashed their bro time. Jesus needs to correct two ways Peter is looking in the wrong direction. The first is looking backward; Peter feels guilt and shame over what he did the night Jesus died.

How does Jesus redirect Peter from looking backward?

Beside the same type of fire where Peter denied Jesus, He is asking him, "Peter, do you love me more than these?" The night before Jesus' crucifixion, Peter insisted he loved Jesus more than any of the other disciples and promised to never deny Jesus, even to death. Jesus is forgiving Peter for denying Him and inviting him to stop living in the past.

After the two of them share this special moment, Jesus tells a bit of what will come for Peter in the future. Specifically, Peter will one day be a martyr.[b] Jesus says, even with this difficulty on the horizon, Peter should, "Follow me!" He wants Peter prepared and encouraged in the difficulties ahead.

---

[a] Jeremiah 2:12-13. God tells the heavens to be amazed and dumbfounded that His people (Israel in this case) had forsaken the true source of life (His living water) for fleeting pleasures that cannot satisfy (broken cisterns that cannot even hold water).

[b] John notes this more explicitly in verse 19 since he is writing with hindsight, most likely after Peter's death.

But Peter doesn't respond with his usual bluster and boasting. Instead, Peter points at John and says, "What about him?" Rather than focus on this moment, where Jesus is inviting him to a deeper commitment, Peter looks around and compares himself to another disciple.

How does Jesus redirect Peter from looking around (comparison)?

Jesus' story has wrapped up, but the next "book" isn't about Jesus. What comes next is all the apostles; what comes next is Peter as the cornerstone of a whole new movement. The Peter we have seen throughout John isn't the Peter we see in the sequels (like Acts). He has been the funny guy; now he will take on the mantle of protagonist. John uses this epilogue, with the bros fishing and a bonus miracle, to set the stage for what comes next.

God's Story in Your Life

So, is that it? Did I add a day to this study to pontificate about epilogues? No, that was just an excuse. I wanted to take this time to tell you how amazing you are. Maybe you finished your book and maybe you didn't. Perhaps you hit your word count goal and perhaps not. Maybe you are crushing this whole living-with-purpose thing and maybe you aren't. Today we looked at the last chapter of John, which is a giant orange highlighter, pointing out how Jesus forgives us when we fall short!

I really wanted to finish writing this study in 30 days, and I didn't make it. (And don't even get me started on the YA fantasy I abandoned at the beginning of week 2.) But God wasn't surprised when I missed my self-imposed deadline. Just like He did with Peter, He pulls my focus away from what I did, or didn't do, and points me toward where He is taking me from here.

Just because you finished your book, or are crushing your purpose, doesn't mean this isn't applicable to you. Satan would love for you to get so excited about what you have done that you forget to keep going. If you keep looking backward, at what you did, you will never look forward, to what God wants to do next. I have said it before and I will say it again and again and again: **If you are still alive, God isn't done with you.**

Whatever mistakes you made are forgiven. Whatever successes you had are only a warm-up. God is using you to do something amazing. If your focus is trapped in the past, you are going to miss it.

What past successes or failures do you keep meditating on? How will you refocus?

Don't make Peter's other mistake either! When another writer gets a book deal, has a successful book launch, or blows away a Kickstarter goal, I can doubt myself. Far too often, I am the runner who can't win her own race because I keep looking at the other runners.

How is comparison distracting you from your purpose? How will you refocus?

Don't look back. Don't look around. Focus on who you are and what God has created you to do. Life isn't a sprint, run in short bursts of focus. This is a marathon. Whether this study helped you get from mile 1 to 2 or from mile 21 to 22, I am so glad to be a cheerleader for you as you run hard after the life God created for you to live.

Daily Tracking Sheet __ / __ / __

Today's writing goal is _____, which I will celebrate by _____.

I will connect with _____, by _____.

I will move my body by _____.

Today's Personal Goals:

1:

2:

3:

Reflection Questions

Today's Biggest Victory:

Today's Biggest Challenge and How I Overcame:

I am grateful for:

1:
2:
3:

Week 6 Discussion and Review

But exhort one another every day, as long as it is called "today," that none of you may be hardened by the deceitfulness of sin. Hebrews 3:13

Story Check-In

Overall, how do you feel about your writing journey? What are the successes and struggles of this experience?

Celebrate with those who hit their goal and encourage those who didn't. It's about writing your story, not meeting an arbitrary timeframe.

Bible Study Check-In

What most surprised you from John 18-21?

What affected you most in this look at Jesus' death and resurrection?

Where do you tend to "look" that distracts you from your purpose (backward or at others)?

How will you maintain the habit of staying in the Word now that this study is ending?

God's Story in Your Life

How have you made progress on your purpose over the last six weeks?

What next steps do you have in pursuing your purpose?

Pray and Close

Thank God for what He taught you in this study and through writing your story.

Thank God for the progress you have all made in pursuing your purpose. Pray for the road ahead.

Pray for the books you have written to be used by God to impact the world. Ask Him to guide you through the editing, publishing, and marketing processes.

My notes and doodles:

God's Epic Story

Before there was anything, there was God.[a] Then He spoke, and His words became reality.[b] His story was perfect. Man and woman existed in perfect harmony, image-bearers of their creator, God.[c]

In His story, we lived in perfect relationship with all things:

- **We lived in harmony with God**, walking and speaking with Him openly.[d]
- **We lived in harmony with one another**, "naked and unashamed" because we had nothing to hide.[e]
- **We lived in harmony with ourselves**, understanding our role as image bearers and free of shame, guilt, pain, or heartache.[f]
- **We lived in harmony with nature**; our role in the story was to tend and care for the world.[g]

But, like every epic story, this was only a beginning. The antagonist of our story came and made us question if life was truly perfect. Satan offered Adam and Eve a choice: to continue trusting in the goodness of God's story or to take control and rewrite the story with themselves at the center.[h] They chose self, and we have been doing the same ever since.[i]

We reach for self-preservation rather than love and self-gratification rather than sacrifice. It is this desire to establish our identity and worth in what we define as good, apart from a relationship with our Maker, that the Bible calls idolatry. A simple definition of idolatry is the worship of created things rather than our Creator God.[j] Idolatry always results in sin, meaning we miss the mark of God's design.[k]

Sin destroys the four relationships God created in perfect harmony:

- **Sin strips us of intimacy with God**.[l] His perfection cannot be with sin; his holiness would utterly destroy us. We live separated from God now and without hope or rest in the afterlife, forever separated from the Giver of all good things.[m]
- **Sin steals our peace with one another** as we jostle and compete for the leading role in this story.[n] Nations rage and war with one another.[o] Individuals lie, cheat, steal, abuse, and use one another in our constant need for more.[p]
- **Sin destroys our relationship with ourselves**. Because we cannot measure up to our design, as bearers of God's image, we ache with a longing we cannot understand or satisfy. We try in vain to fill the insatiable void within us with sex, drugs, food, social media, money, or anything else we can get our hands on. What promises to satisfy only leaves us broken, ashamed, and empty.[q]
- **Sin corrupts nature**; our world is no longer a paradise.[r] We destroy creation by fighting to be at the center of the story. Instead of cultivating the world God created for us, we mishandle, exploit, strip of resources, and destroy nature in our insatiable quest for more.[s]

There is still hope. God spoke in the garden, in the moment of our original sin, of His promised champion.[t] He sent prophets and teachers throughout the Old Testament to prepare our hearts for His coming Messiah.[u] Then He did the unthinkable: He stepped into the brokenness of our story.

God became human, as Jesus of Nazareth. He stripped away His own divinity, humbled Himself to don human flesh, and lived among us in our broken world.[v] He loves us so much,[w] and wants us to know His love personally, so the Creator of all things took on a body susceptible to pain, heartache, brokenness, and death.[x]

---

[a] Genesis 1:1a
[b] Genesis 1:3
[c] Genesis 1:27
[d] Genesis 1:28-30, 2:15-17
[e] Genesis 2:25
[f] Genesis 2:25
[g] Genesis 2:15
[h] Genesis 3:4-5
[i] Genesis 3:6
[j] Romans 1:22-25
[k] Romans 3:23
[l] Genesis 3:8b-10
[m] Isaiah 59:2
[n] Genesis 3:7
[o] James 4:1-2
[p] Romans 1:28-32
[q] Galatians 5:19-21
[r] Genesis 3:17b-18
[s] Romans 8:20-22
[t] Genesis 3:15b
[u] John 5:39-40
[v] John 1:15
[w] John 3:16-17
[x] Philippians 2:5-8

Jesus modeled for us what a true image-bearer looks like. He showed us how to live in perfect relationship with God, each other, ourselves, and nature. He taught us to pray for God's kingdom to come to earth and showed us how to live out His work of restoration.

Then He went further. After living the perfect life we cannot live, he took on the death we each deserve.[a] Jesus became like us so that we could become like Him.[b] After a sinless life,[c] He swapped places with us, dying a brutal death on a Roman cross.[d] In His sacrifice, He paid the debt we could never pay[e] and purchased for us the eternal life that we do not deserve.[f]

But death had no right to Jesus and could not hold Him long. In the ultimate plot twist, Jesus wrested the keys of hell from death and rose from the grave.[g] Through His death, we find forgiveness for our sin. In His resurrection, we receive the power to restore the brokenness that sin brought into the world.

God does not force this choice on any of us.[h] Jesus paid the debt; we must choose to accept His gift of freedom and salvation. In doing so, He reconnects our hearts to the heart of our Creator, and we become new beings.[i] We have no role in our salvation;[j] it's not about the good works we can do.[k] We bring our brokenness to Him and He makes us whole.[l]

From our new identity, through the power of the Holy Spirit, He empowers us to join in God's work of reconciliation:[m]

- **We have restored intimacy with God.**[n] Jesus strips away the sin separating us from God, allowing us to live in harmony with God and look forward to an eternity in His presence.[o] We work to restore others to relationship with God by sharing this Good News.[p]
- **We have peace with one another.**[q] No longer in competition for the role of protagonist, we encourage, support, and collaborate with one another. Considering God's forgiveness, we forgive others.[r] This mosaic of generations, ethnicities, and cultures finds unified purpose in His story of reconciliation.[s]
- **We live at peace with ourselves.**[t] We are no longer left wallowing in condemnation and shame, seeking something to fill the void inside. God wiped our slate clean and empowers us to imitate Jesus in living as image-bearers of the divine God.[u]
- **We restore nature.** We recognize our responsibility to steward God's creation and collaborate to restore, nurture, and care for the natural world.[v]

The Good News of the Gospel is not that God will snatch us away from this dreadful place called earth. The Good News is that, through His people, God is telling a new story that is restoring our world right now.

Throughout the 30 days of Writing Your Story With God we examined the story God is writing with your life. When we zoom out, we realize your story is only one subplot in the epic adventure that He is writing in the World. This is His story of redemption, of old things becoming new, and of dead things coming back to life. This is the story of you, His image-bearing creation, realizing who He created you to be and partnering with Him to live your purpose of restoring humanity to God's original design.

The Author of the greatest story ever told is inviting you to play a part in this unfolding plot of redemption. However, it is your choice to accept this invitation. To do so, simply cry out, "Jesus, rescue me."[w] Confess your need for Jesus' death to forgive your sins and His resurrection to empower your restoration. Jump wholeheartedly into His mission of reconciliation and choose to make Him the Author of your story from this day forward.[25]

---

[a] 1 Corinthians 15:22
[b] 2 Corinthians 5:21
[c] Hebrews 4:15
[d] Romans 6:23
[e] Isaiah 53:5-6
[f] Romans 5:12,18-19
[g] 1 Corinthians 15:3-4
[h] John 3:36
[i] 2 Corinthains 5:17
[j] Romans 5:8
[k] 2 Timothy 1:9
[l] Ephesians 2:8-9
[m] 2 Corinthians 5:18-20
[n] Romans 8:38-39
[o] Ephesians 2:14-16
[p] Matthew 28:19-20
[q] Luke 6:27-28
[r] Ephesians 4:31-32
[s] Galatians 3:27-28
[t] 1 John 1:9
[u] Romans 8:1-2
[v] Mark 16:15
[w] Romans 10:9-10

Glossary

1st Person: a writing style where the story is told by the protagonist, identifiable by its use of "I" and "we" pronouns. We see this style in *To Kill a Mockingbird* and *The Adventures of Huckleberry Fin*.

2nd Person: a writing style where the story is told to the protagonist, identifiable by its use of "you" pronouns. We see this style in *The Night Circus* and most Choose Your Own Adventure books.

3rd Person: a writing style where the story is told by an uninvolved third party, identifiable by the lack of "I," "we," or "you" pronouns (outside of dialogue). We see this style in *Harry Potter* and *Pride and Prejudice*.

3rd Person Limited: a version of the 3rd person writing style where the perspective is limited to a character's perspective. These stories can follow a single character (like in *Harry* Potter) but more often cycle between two or more Point of View (POV) characters. We see this style in *Game of Thrones* and *The Lord of the Rings*.

3rd Person Omniscient: a version of the 3rd person writing style where the narrator knows all. We see this style in *The Scarlet Letter* and *Dune*.

A Story: the primary plot line for a book or other narrative work. This is the external action where the protagonist goes after what they believe will fix their problem.

B Story: the story that runs parallel to the primary plotline (A Story) and reflects an internal transformation in the protagonist as they become who they need to be to fix their real problem.

Backstory: what happened to the protagonist before the story began.

Beat: term Blake Snyder used to define a plot point.

Beat Sheet: a way of outlining a story by identifying the 15 "beats" (from the BS2) that make up the core of its structure.

BS2 / Blake Snyder Beat Sheet: first introduced in Blake Snyder's book, *Save the Cat!*, this structure uses 15 beats to outline the major movements in a story. Blake originally based the structure on how to write an effective screenplay. Jessica Brody later adapted it for work specifically with novels in her book *Save the Cat! Writes a Novel*. The BS2 is compared to other plot structures in the Appendix.

Call to Adventure: common term used to refer to the spark that sends a story in a new direction. Interchangeable with Catalyst (Day 4) or inciting incident.

Chekhov's gun: a narrative principle first outlined by Anton Checkov that states, "If you say in the first chapter that there is a rifle hanging on the wall, in the second or third chapter it absolutely must go off. If it's not going to be fired, it shouldn't be hanging there." The goal is to ensure that all story elements an author sets up receive a proper payoff before the story ends.

Climax: in most story structures, this is the high-stakes moment at the end of the story when all plot points come into alignment, also known as the Finale. Freytag, however, used this term to refer to the Midpoint Twist when the story goes in a new direction.

Exposition: explaining information to the reader about setting, people, characters, and backstory. Done well, it adds richness and meaning to a story. Done poorly, it can destroy immersion for the reader.

***External*[a] Problem**: what the protagonist sees as an issue in their life.

Falling Action: also called resolution, this comes after the Climax or Finale to tie up loose story threads.

---

[a] External is in italics because it is optional. When "problem" is used in writing circles without clarifying "internal" or "external," it refers to their external problem.

138 | Glossary

Fatal Flaw: the character flaw that the protagonist must address. Other terms include Internal Problem or shard of glass.

Fear: the deep, soul crushing fear that our protagonist will do anything to avoid. This fear is backed up by a misbelief that grew out of their backstory. Overcoming this fear will take learning their life lesson.

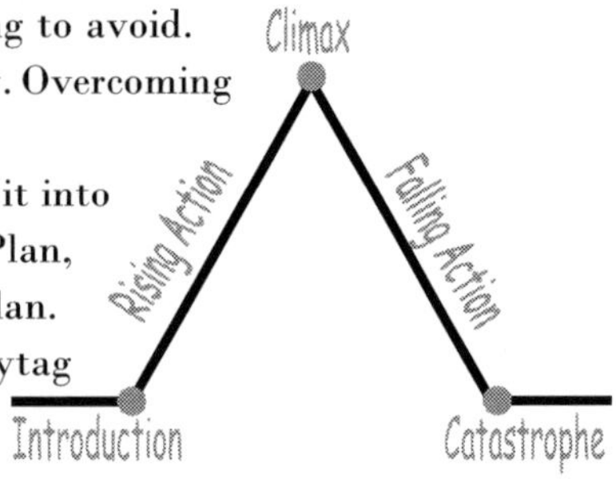

Five Point Finale: Blake Snyder's approach to the Finale, by breaking it into five points. The five points are Gathering the Team, Executing the Plan, High Tower Surprise, Dig Deep Down, and Execution of the New Plan.

Freytag's Pyramid: one of the oldest documented plot structures, Freytag based his famous pyramid on the central premise of a midpoint twist, which he called the Climax. The Appendix compares Freytag's Pyramid to other plot structures.

Genre: the category for an artistic work. Can refer to broad categories (Fantasy) or be narrowed down to an ultra-specific subgenre (Young Adult Paranormal Fantasy Romance) and anywhere in between. Genres tend to come with their own unique Tropes and audience expectations.

Goal: what the protagonist believes (usually incorrectly) will solve their problem. Also referred to as their want.

Hero's Journey: popularized by the book *A Hero with 1,000 Faces*, this plot structure is drawn as a circle. The hero leaves their Ordinary World because of a Call to Adventure, goes into the Special World, where he endures trials and tests, then emerges back into the Ordinary World as an improved person. The Appendix compares the Hero's Journey to other plot structures.

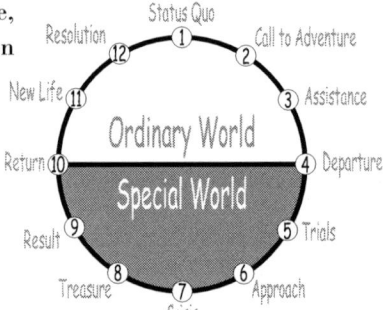

Inciting Incident: common term used to refer to the spark that sends a story in a new direction. Interchangeable with Catalyst (discussed on day 4) or Call to Adventure.

Internal Problem: the character flaw that the protagonist must address. Other terms include Shard of Glass or Fatal Flaw.

Life Lesson: the internal transformation that will solve the protagonist's real (internal) problem. Also referred to as their Need.

MacGuffin: a story element that has no impact on the story aside from serving as an item to move the plot along. One example would be the Philosopher's Stone in *Harry Potter*.

Meet Cute: the delightful or amusing first meeting of future romantic partners in a romance story.

Misbelief: the untrue statement the protagonist holds on to as fact because of trauma in their backstory. Because of this misbelief, they have a fear they can only overcome by learning the life lesson that contradicts this misbelief.

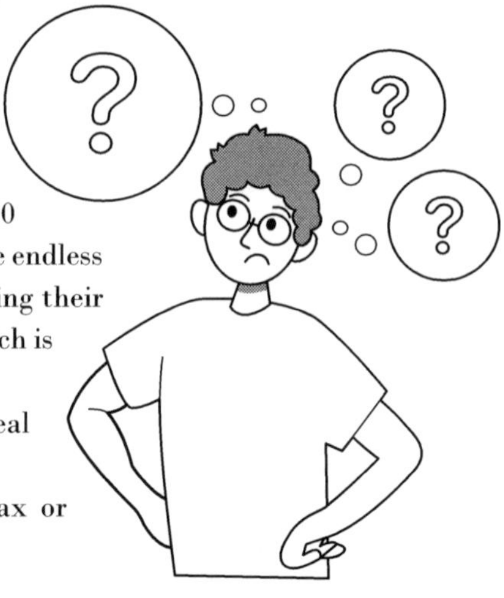

Mood: the overall feel of a story.

NaNoWriMo: National Novel Writing Month. Every November, NaNoWriMo challenges participants to write 50,000 words in 30 days. The focus is on getting the story on paper and avoiding the endless loop of restarts and rewrites that keep many people from finishing their stories. NaNoWriMo also hosts "Camp NaNo" twice a year, which is a scaled-down version of the November event.

Need: the internal transformation that will solve the protagonist's real (internal) problem. Also referred to as the Life Lesson.

Resolution: also called Falling Action, this comes after the Climax or Finale to tie up loose story threads.

Shard of Glass: the character flaw that the protagonist must address. Other terms include Internal Problem or Fatal Flaw.

Story Triangle: story structure based on Freytag's Pyramid, but with modern language. Usually depicted as an asymmetrical triangle, shifting the Climax to the end, instead of at the Midpoint, as in Freytag's original design.

Style: the way an author structures their book. For example, *Dracula* is written as a series of diary entries. Another stylistic choice would be the point of view (1st, 2nd, or 3rd person).

Theme: the point the author is communicating to his or her audience; usually synonymous with the protagonist's Need.

Three Act Structure: this plot structure breaks a story into three acts. We credit Aristotle with defining the Three Act Structure, but multiple writers have since developed their own versions. Most modern plot structures borrow elements, or lift entirely, from the Three Act Structure. Because so many distinct versions exist, this structure is very flexible and can map to almost any narrative. The appendix compares the Three Act Structure to other plot structures.

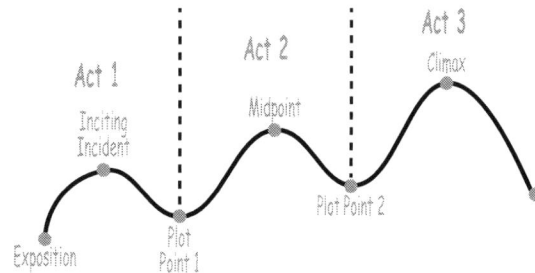

Tone: the attitude an author conveys with their choice of sentence structure, word choice, and punctuation.

Trope: term used to describe commonly occurring literary or rhetorical devices, cliches, and motifs. For example, "enemies to lovers" is a trope found in many Romance genres.

Unreliable Narrator: a technique where the narrator gives wrong information to the reader, either on purpose or by accident. Famous books with unreliable narrators include *Life of Pi*, *Gone Girl*, and *Fight Club*.

Want: what the protagonist believes (usually incorrectly) will solve their problem. Also referred to as their goal.

Add your own terms for quick reference:

Appendix

There are hundreds of different plot structures available; I chose these four because they provide a good sample of what you will find on the topic. Each looks better as a picture, especially the Hero's Journey. I present them below as lists to show how they compare, sacrificing clarity in the process.

Learn more about each structure by visiting the YouTube playlist I created for each (scan the QR code to access an online version of this page with live links). These playlists are ever-improving as I find more videos on each structure. You can recommend videos to add to any of these playlists by sharing them with me via email or through any of my social media accounts.

Find sketches of The Hero's Journey, Freytag's Pyramid, and an approach to Three Act Structure in the Glossary.

		Blake Snyder Beat Sheet		**Three Act Structure**		**The Hero's Journey**		**Freytag's Pyramid** *(Story Triangle)*
Beats / Scenes / Plot Points	**Act 1**	Opening Image	**Ascending Action**	**Act 1** *Setup*	Beginning	**Ordinary**	Status Quo	Exposition
		Theme Stated						
		Setup						
		Catalyst			Inciting Incident		Call to Adventure	Inciting Incident
		Debate			Second Thoughts		Assistance	
	Act 2	Break Into 2		**Climax of Act One**			Departure	Rising Action
		B Story		**Act 2** *Confrontation*	Obstacle	**Special World**	Trials	
		Fun and Games			Obstacle		Approach	
		Midpoint			Midpoint Twist		Crisis	Climax [a]
		Bad Guys Close In			Obstacle		Treasure	
		All is Lost			Disaster		Result	Falling Action *Protagonist wrestles with the Climax*
		Dark Night of the Soul			Crisis		Return	
	Act 3	Break Into 3	**Descending Action**	**Climax of Act Two**		**Ordinary**		
		Five Point Finale		**Act 3** *Resolution*	Climax of Act 3		New Life	Catastrophe
					Wrap Up			Dénouement [b] *Optional*
		Final Image			End		Resolution	
Notes		Originally Developed for Film by Blake Snyder and published in his *Save the Cat!* book. For this reason, writers often call this the "Save the Cat" structure.		There are hundreds of ways "Three Act Structure" is defined and a variety of terms are used. I used one of the most popular. This is the most adapted of the structures listed here.		Better understood as a circle (see the picture in the glossary). My effort here is to align the terms with other structures.		Typically used for tragedies, which begin with rising hope and end in catastrophe, although these ideas can be used in other story types.
📖		*Save the Cat! Save the Cat! Writes a Novel*		There is no one book that is the definitive guide. Many attribute the structure to Aristotle but its true origins are unknown.		*Hero With 1000 Faces*		*Freytag's Technique of the Drama*
▶		The BS2		Three Act Structure		Hero's Journey		Freytag's Pyramid
🔗		savethecat.com		nownovel.com/blog/three-act-formula-novels/		blog.reedsy.com/guide/story-structure/heros-journey		stormwritingschool.com/freytags-pyramid/

---

[a] Here this word is used to refer to the change in direction that modern writers call a Midpoint Twist.

[b] French word (since Freytag was French) that refers to all the closing scenes at the end of a story, after the main event (Catastrophe) has happened. This is optional because in many plays, which were his primary inspiration, the Catastrophe was the last scene.

Dedication and Acknowledgments

I dedicate this book to these amazing people who made it possible.

To my family:

Mom, we did it! You were always a fierce supporter of my dreams of becoming a writer. I remember late nights together working on timelines or planning character arcs. You meticulously edited nearly everything I wrote for several years. I couldn't have finished this marathon without you, even though I had to run the last mile by myself. I wish you could be here to see me cross the finish line.

Daddy, I know you would be so proud. Thank you for always believing in my dreams, no matter what they were. You raised all four of us to live disciplined, responsible lives. But you also instilled in me a love for Bible study and modeled consistent prayer. I think often of those moments catching you praying at 2:30 in the morning or reading the Bible before anyone else in the camper woke up.

Matt, thank you for pushing me to always keep improving. **Russell**, your excitement over the story you are writing rekindled my passion when it grew cold. **Cassie**, not only were you an amazing Beta reader, you were also my only proofreader. I love how much closer we have grown by working on this project together.

Princess Jasmine is my adorable, spoiled rotten, tiny, furry overlord. For years, I rolled my eyes at pet owners who treated their animals like family. Then you showed up. You were only supposed to stay for a few weeks until I went back to work. But as the lockdowns continued, you snuggled your way into my life and then into my heart. Now I cannot imagine life without you.

To my community:

Thank you to all the Alpha and Beta readers, who provided feedback, and to the amazing community of people God has blessed me with in this season. I am passionate about the power of community because it transformed my life. God did not create us to do life alone!

- **Amanda M**, your insight transformed the structure of this study between the first and second draft. Thank you for carving out time to provide feedback while juggling all your family, church, and work commitments.
- **Amanda W**, thank you for your insight and diligent study of the Word of God.
- **Aunt Diane**, thank you for all the encouraging notes in those early days when I wanted to toss the whole study.
- **Aunt Kathy**, thank you for encouraging me throughout the process and for everything you do to take care of Bonnie.
- **Chris and Joey**, your faithfulness and servants' hearts inspire me to action. Thank you for the practical ways you love me.
- **Courtney and Will**, thank you for welcoming me and giving me a place to belong when I felt untethered.
- **Elena**, you are a delight and light up every room you enter. Keep using that influence God gave you!
- **Glenda and Jim**, your wisdom and insight bless our community, and your commitment to each other inspires us all.
- **Gloria and Jerome**, thank you for being the hands of Jesus, despite enduring personal disappointment.
- **Justin**, you are an amazing man of God. Your character provides a firm foundation for our community.
- **Kaitlyn**, you have taught me what it means to be a true friend, both when it's easy and when it's hard. Thank you for encouraging me to take up space in your life.
- **Katina**, thank you for your encouragement and prayers.

142 | Dedication and Acknowledgments

- **Kristina**, thank you for providing feedback from an author's perspective and for helping me plan the book launch.
- **Maria**, thank you for teaching me the power of friendship and how to slow down and enjoy life.
- **Michael**, you inspire me with your openness as you fight to break strongholds. Stay in the process; God is writing an amazing story with your life!
- **Nick**, you bring a joy and youthfulness we all need. When you are gone, your absence is felt.
- **Nicole**, your steadiness inspires me to keep going no matter what happens. Thank you for being a constant cheerleader for myself and others, even when God's timing doesn't seem fair.
- **Pastor Brett**, thank you for providing a framework to help me articulate the Gospel so perfectly. We create as image bearers of the Author who wrote the greatest story ever told!
- **Stephen and Rebecca**, thank you for your Biblical insight, constant prayer, and ongoing encouragement. I appreciate the many years of wisdom and guidance; my life will never be the same.
- **Swami**, I love how willing you are to try new things and how you push me outside my comfort zone.
- **Tranise**, thank you for the unique perspective you provided on the first draft of this manuscript and for helping me plan the book launch.
- The whole **Woodard Community Group**! We are growing so fast that on each draft I add more names to this list! I look forward to getting to know you all better as we continue pursuing God together. Thank you for loving and serving each other well!

To Aunt Patti:

I especially want to thank **Aunt Patti**. Without you, I would never have written this study. After my parents died, you became a mother to me. We laughed together, cried together, and spent hours talking about a lot of nothing.

I will never forget finishing my first blog after mom's death and not knowing what to do. Mom was my proofreader, and she was gone. You've never corrected my commas or reworded my sentences. But letting me read that blog to you, and many others after it, helped me continue writing.

You encouraged me to take this writing thing seriously, helped me out of writing slumps, reminded me to take breaks, and continued supporting me, no matter how many fictional characters I murdered.

When Imposter Syndrome is eating my lunch, you remind me this is God's project, and He's got this. When I am stuck in any story, you are the one I call to talk through the plot and figure out what to do next. No matter how many times you tell me you are "just an accountant," your questions and ideas always give me the nudge I need to get back on track.

Thank you, Patti. I love you.

Dedication and Acknowledgments | 143

#NotSponsored... but thank you!

This is #NotSponsored. But I wanted to give a hearty "thank you" to these fantastic organizations and individuals who helped make Writing Your Story With God a reality.

- **4TheWords** uses gamification to help writers write more without distraction. I slayed many "monsters," and completed many quests while writing this book. The 4TheWords Discord is also a great place to go for inspiration and community.
- **Celeste** provided the final line edit. Her feedback put a layer of polish on this book to help it become what you hold in your hands.
- **Crossway** provides an open license for the English Standard Version (ESV). This allowed me to include scripture quotations without needing to go through an approval process. I use ESV for my personal Bible study because it balances staying true to the original texts and using common language that is easy to understand.
- **Dena**'s cabins in the Smokey Mountains provided the perfect getaway to finish editing this book. The cabins are charming and cozy, offering the ideal escape from my hectic Austin lifestyle. Patti and I have started a tradition of staying in the bear cabin every spring.
- **Katerina**, my illustrator, perfectly captured the creative and playful vision I had for this study. Working with her has been a pleasure.
- **Kris**, we couldn't be more different, but we still have an excellent relationship. Thank you for supporting my dreams, both practically and emotionally.
- **Lofi Girl**'s music was exactly what I needed to boost my concentration when working on this manuscript. Additionally, Lofi Girl gives small creators, like me, access to quality music for their YouTube videos.
- **NaNoWriMo**, which you already know if you've read the study, affected me more than I can explain. I always wanted to be an author. But, without NaNoWriMo, I might still be planning to "someday" write a book. Thank you for giving me the push to sit down and make serious progress.
- **ProWritingAid** is the software I used for multiple passes of editing and proofreading. It also improves my writing in other spheres, like work, because it integrates with tools like Outlook and Word. Specifically, I cannot say enough about how much I love the new Rephrase feature! I'm grateful there's no limit to how many times you can use Rephrase, because I'd hit the cap every day.
- **Round Rock Writer's Guild**, thank you for providing a welcoming and supportive environment for writers at every skill level.
- Before clarifying my vision, I hired **Shoon** to illustrate the companion journal. Although Katerina's illustrations are in *Journaling through John*, I included clips of Shoon's art in this study. You can download PDFs of Shoon's coloring pages on my website.

Check out Shoon's art and other resources.

About the Author

My life purpose is to *encourage, empower, and equip the sleepwalking children of God to break free of strongholds and pursue their dreams*.[a] Let me explain what all those words mean to me and why this is the purpose statement that centers everything I do.

- **Encourage**: inspire believers to identify their purpose and encourage them to pursue it.
- **Empower**: provide training that empowers believers with the confidence and direction to take action.
- **Equip**: supply tools, resources, and funding that equips believers to progress in their purpose.
- **Sleepwalking**: sound the alarm to wake up God's sleeping children to live lives of purpose. This generation, more than any generation before, has been lulled to sleep by a world of distractions.
- **Children of God**: recognize my calling is first-and-foremost to believers.[b] Salvation is not enough; we are called to live for Christ. What comes after salvation is where my gifts, talents, and passions most align.
- **Break Free of Strongholds**: Unhealed hurts, unhealthy habits, and unaddressed hangups leave us vulnerable to the Enemy and limit our ability to live with purpose.
- **Pursue their Dreams**: God created every person with purpose. We are all born with dreams, but the world and life will often bury them. My purpose is to help believers get out a shovel to dig those dreams up, clean them off, and then get to work making them reality.

Sometimes my purpose plays out in a conversation one on one. Other times, it is speaking at an event or writing a book. Each season looks different, but my underlying purpose remains consistent. Micro or macro, these are the principles that guide me to live life on purpose.

This passion for encouraging, empowering, and equipping resonates throughout my life, even though this clearly defined purpose wasn't articulated until my late 20's. Various adults encouraged this ambition by giving me chances to use my talents with supervision in safe environments. I fondly remember teaching different Sunday school classes throughout elementary and middle school. And my debut as a public speaker was in 8th grade, when I gave a 15-minute "sermon" in chapel – twice!

In high school and college, I became more active in forming communities structured around studying the Bible and connecting with God. Now I am more focused on helping people recognize and live their purpose, while still teaching the Word when given the chance. The comfort and convenience of our culture has lulled too many to sleep. I want to wake them up, train them, and send them out to live lives that really matter.

Thank you for letting me be a footnote in the epic story God is writing with your life. Connect with me on social media or subscribe to my newsletter for updates as I pursue this life of purpose.

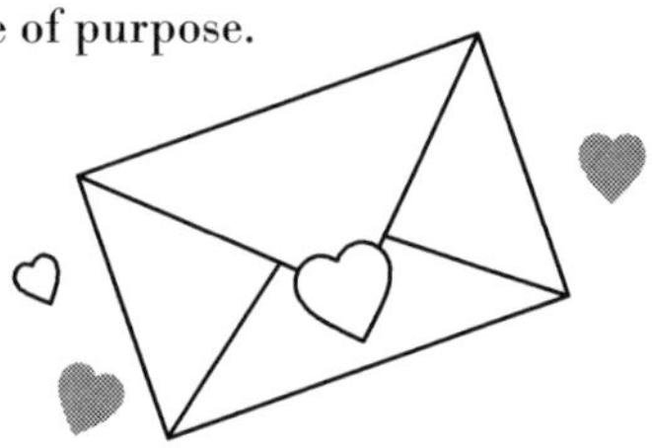

ImperfectProgressTitles.com/Newsletter
Facebook.com/ProgressingImperfectly
Instagram.com/ProgressingImperfectly/
Twitter.com/NperfectProgres
YouTube.com/channel/ProgressingImperfectly

---

[a] This purpose statement took several years to develop but began with reading the book *The 7 Habits of Highly Effective People* by Stephen Covey.

[b] All believers are called to be a light to the world and prepared to share our story with nonbelievers. I am not exception. But my primary calling is to believers, and this is where I focus my time, attention, and resources.

Endnotes

Access these endnotes on my website by scanning the QR code or typing in the link below.

ImperfectProgressTitles.com/References

---

[1] According to nanowrimo.org/about-nano, in 2022, 413,295 writers participated in NaNoWriMo and 51,670 "won" by hitting the goal.
[2] wikiwrimo.org/wiki/NaNoWriMo_statistics
[3] thebooknetwork.co.uk/the-blog/13-nanowrimo-books-that-have-been-published#:~:text=But%20she%20isn't%20the,smaller%20presses%20or%20self%2Dpublished.
[4] https://collected.jcu.edu/cgi/viewcontent.cgi?article=1055&context=mastersessays#
[5] Save The Cat! pages xv-xvi and 120-123.
[6] realfaith.com/sermons/angry-jesus-cleanses-the-temple/
[7] workingpreacher.org/commentaries/narrative-lectionary/cleansing-the-temple/commentary-on-john-213-25-2
[8] vimeo.com/274418019?embedded=true&source=video_title&owner=63205691
[9] colinshope.org/about-us/colins-story/
[10] etymonline.com/word/*ag-#etymonline_v_52549
[11] blog.adw.org/wp-content/uploads/2018/03/37-Miracles-of-Jesus-in-Chronological-Order.pdf My count excludes sign #37, since we are specifically looking at during his ministry (AKA before his death and resurrection).
[12] hebrew4christians.com/Scripture/Torah/Oral_Torah/oral_torah.html
[13] ohr.edu/ask_db/ask_main.php/39/Q1/
[14] All 10 of the Commandments can be tied up in these two commands. philgons.com/2021/01/how-do-love-for-god-and-love-for-others-relate-the-two-greatest-commands-as-one/#the-ten-commandments
[15] jewishroots.net/library/holiday-articles/water_libation_ceremony.html (The source's underline I have replaced with bold.) Read the full article; I promise it's worth it!
[16] Read more about that here: lucris.lub.lu.se/ws/portalfiles/portal/57820558/Court_of_the_Gentiles_m_fr.pdf
[17] gracetranscendingthetorah.com/scrolls/writing-gods-name/
[18] biblestudytools.com/bible-study/topical-studies/why-it-matters-that-god-is-yahweh.html
[19] It's a bit long but this teaching is excellent on the idea of God's self-existence. sljinstitute.net/systematic-theology/theology-proper/attributes-of-god-part-ii-where-did-god-come-from-or-the-self-existence-of-god/
[20] corechristianity.com/resource-library/articles/three-differences-gods-self-existence-makes-every-day/
[21] letthewordsflow.wordpress.com/2011/05/12/narrative-tension-and-the-ticking-clock/
[22] Like this one: screencraft.org/blog/101-plot-twist-ideas/
[23] jerichowriters.com/how-to-write-a-compelling-plot-twist-a-complete-guide/
[24] Read more about Pilate after Jesus's death in this article: historytoday.com/history-matters/strange-afterlife-pontius-pilate
[25] Learn more about God's epic story: https://youtube.com/playlist?list=PL7H38SxVUvlmTwb2_0iwkH59cIGJQqiJg

Word Count Tracker

How many words you write is not a measure of your success or value as an author. Remember, my first NaNoWriMo I wrote over 140k words and amounted to nothing! That said, setting goals can help break down a larger project into something more manageable. If having a word count goal helps you, then do it. If having a word count goal hinders you. Don't do it!

Choose Your Word Count Goal

Just because the NaNoWriMo official goal is 50,000 words, does not mean that is the right goal for you. Many factors influence how long your book should be, including audience, genre, and the dictates of your specific story. The length of your first draft usually differs from your finished book based on your personality. As an "over-writer," my manuscripts shrink in editing as I strip out all the excess words. But "under-writers" fill in more detail on their second draft. Instead of letting what works for others affect your manuscript or your self-esteem, show yourself kindness by focusing on your own goals.

What is your word count goal?

Divide your goal by 100 and write it in the sign at the top of the wall.[a]

The word count tracking graphic breaks your goal down into 100 steps with milestones along the way. There is a step (or steppingstone) for each % of your goal. So, 500 words per step for a 50,000 word goal.

Identify your rewards

Along the way to your goal, take some time to celebrate your progress. I had Katerina use landings (and a bridge) for the 10% 30%, 50%, 70%, and 90% and doors to represent the 20%, 40%, 60%, and 80% milestones. There is also a landing halfway to the stretch goal. These are chances for you to pause and enjoy the view. Consider small rewards, like an hour reading your favorite book, a bubble bath, or a fancy coffee. Even if you will to continue toward a stretch goal, don't forget to celebrate big when you achieve your goal!

Use the table below to set your milestones and identify your rewards.

Milestone	Words	Reward
10%		
20		
30		
40		
50		
60		
70		
80		
90		
Complete!		
½ to Strech		
Stretch Goal		

[a] If you have a stretch goal, divide the number of extra words by 20 to calculate the ladder rungs.

Made in United States
Orlando, FL
03 October 2023

37536570R00083